DAY CARE PERSONNEL MANAGEMENT

Nancy Travis and Joe Perreault

Day Care Personnel Management was first published as part of the Training for Child Care Project, which was carried out at the Southern Regional Education Board, Atlanta, Georgia, with support from the Carnegie Corporation and the Levi Strauss Foundation. When the project at the Southern Regional Education Board was completed, the work of the project was continued by the Child Care Support Center, a part of Save the Children's Southern States Office. Therefore, this publication is now printed under the auspices of the Child Care Support Center.

ISBN 0-940292-00-9

Distributed by
Gryphon House, Inc.
P.O. Box 217
Mt. Rainier, MD 20822

Table of Contents

Introduction

The Child Care Support Center promotes quality day care by developing administrative skills of day care directors. The center has explored with day care leaders almost all aspects of administration and has developed workshops and training materials for directors.

From this experience we have identified a number of administrative skills which need to be built into the ongoing training of all day care directors. One of the most important of these subjects is personnel management. Competent, satisfied employees are an essential ingredient in any enterprise, but they are of special importance in the human services such as child care.

The Importance of Employees

Day care is a labor intensive industry; personnel costs in day care usually constitute from 60 to 80 percent of a program's budget. At the same time, most day care, whether provided through a for profit or a not-for-profit organization, operates on a slim financial margin. The day care program must carefully balance between the ability of parents or third party funding sources to pay for the cost of child care and the need to compensate staff for their labor and their constant concern for children. Thus, decisions regarding how much staff is required, how to utilize staff, and how much to pay for salaries and fringe benefits can have a significant effect on the quality of the program and on whether or not a given day care program will survive.

Role of the Day Care Director

Most day care directors have some postsecondary education, often a degree in child development or early childhood education. Their training prepares them for effective work with young children in a classroom setting. Often, after a period of successful teaching, they are promoted to be the director of an entire center. This is an appropriate career advancement which carries with it increases in both income and responsibility. Yet, their preparation leaves gaps in the knowledge and skills of management needed to be administrators.

Fortunately, most people dedicated to child development possess good interpersonal skills. Many of the principles of promoting good will and growth among children have equal application in working with adults. However, most day care directors must acquire some new competencies. Directors must learn how to achieve results through the work of others; they must learn how to confront a wide array of employee personal problems. They must develop an ability to give support and counsel to employees and at the same time be able to separate the personal needs of the employee from the needs of the center to operate effectively. Just as important as developing relationship skills, day care directors need help in establishing a rational plan for personnel management activities. Carefully thought-out and clearly written policies and procedures related to all aspects of the employer/employee relationship constitute a form of preventive supervision and provide the basis for fair treatment of all kinds of employee concerns.

Personnel Management in Day Care is designed to focus on the knowledge, skills, values, and attitudes needed to create an effective work environment. It should be useful to day care directors, supervisory staff, owners and members of boards of directors who must understand and manage this responsibility. Hopefully, the publication will be valuable reading for direct service employees too. The chapters which follow describe the complex pressures and problems of day care employers related to personnel issues and explain with equal concern the needs of day care employees for satisfying careers, as well as personal and financial security.

Information included in the publication was suggested by day care directors who participated in Training for Child Care sponsored workshops on administration, as well as from selected readings and source materials.

CHAPTER 1

Personnel Management in Day Care: An Overview

To provide effective leadership to employees in day care, a broad understanding of four general areas is required. These are:

- The nature of day care and child development and how employees are a resource to achieve these ends.
- Management practices designed to instruct or govern the employer/employee relationship.
- General awareness of styles of management, as well as specific concepts related to supervision and motivation of staff.
- External social and economic factors which influence day care work and employees' view of their work life.

Day Care and Child Development

Individual beliefs about child development, as well as specific child care needs in a given community, will determine many of the important questions of the ways in which staff at a given day care program will be organized and used. These questions include: What will be the role of each staff member? What level of education and experience will be required? Will support staff be needed (e.g., social service or transportation workers)? Will staggered shifts be required, and how will they be scheduled? How will the work day and week be organized? And to some degree, what will be the ratio of staff to children?

As important as these decisions are, they will not be given close attention in this publication because most centers have staff or board members with expertise in questions of program philosophy or design, and all centers have access to a wide, although sometimes conflicting, body of professional literature to help build a plan for operation of the center and deployment of staff.

Furthermore, the design of most centers is based on a commitment to the needs of children and families. Employees are hired partly because they share this belief. Yet, managers of day care programs often assume that a shared commitment to children will result in good employer/employee relationships. While this is frequently true, there are times when the needs of children and families will conflict with the needs of employees. A center which hopes to survive and to preserve the quality of its program must learn how to maintain a balance between these two needs.

Personnel Management Practices

A more necessary starting point for understanding personnel management in day care is a thorough review of basic theory and methods used in the management of employees in any organization. Personnel management tools, such as an operations manual, personnel policies, job descriptions, employment applications, and personnel files, are a required framework for effective employer/employee relationships. Techniques for the recruitment, interviewing, selection, and orientation of new employees, or for the development of employee programs, such as a salary or fringe benefit plan, are often available in programs designed for large business and industrial employers, or through books and periodicals devoted exclusively to personnel management issues. However, few directors have been able to find the time or resources to bridge the gap between sources of knowledge and the particular application to day care.

It is true that many programs have policy statements related to most aspects of the employer/employee relationship and perform most of the required personnel functions. However, this accomplishment is likely to be the product of a random effort spurred by the need to answer a number of specific employee questions or requests. While all of the pieces exist, they have not been woven in a comprehensive fashion nor do they state clearly the employer's overall philosophy toward employees. Chapters 2 through 6 in this publication are devoted to the understanding and development of specific personnel practices.

Supervision and Leadership Skills

Just as important as mastering the policy and procedural aspects of personnel management, an effective day care employer must be an effective supervisor. Good supervision involves skills in interpersonal relationships—an ability more easily acquired through interaction with people than by reading. Supervision also involves understanding employee motivation, providing supervisory conferences and opportunities for employee evaluation and staff development, dealing with employee grievances, and working with employees whose performance is unsatisfactory.

Most of these issues will be addressed in Chapter 7. At the same time, effective personnel management depends on an overall set of beliefs about management and the way authority should be exercised. When the day care program is set up, decisions are made about distribution of authority among parents, board of directors or owners, the director, and employees. The range of possible ways to distribute responsibility is enormous, but each conveys a point-of-view about the capability and expectations of employees. Once the operation begins, the day-to-day contact between director and staff involves a constant expression of beliefs about the role and value of staff. For example, the day care director must decide when, how, and what to communicate to staff: How often should staff be brought together for personal discussion? When are written communications most effective and when are they too impersonal? What information should be conveyed to all staff, to supervisory staff only, or not at all? Each of these decisions conveys an important, although often unstated, message to employees about their individual worth and capacity to contribute to the good of the organization. Decisions which directly affect employees' well being are particularly significant. The amount of information and suggestions an employer seeks from staff before implementing a change in personnel policies will be apparent. Sometimes a shortage of time or other constraint requires that employee input be limited; however an effective day care employer would want to acknowledge such constraints to staff.

These and other characteristics of employer leadership are mentioned throughout the publication.

Social and Economic Climate for Day Care Work

Strengthening the internal management of day care programs through sound personnel procedures and a planned supervisory process should result in improved work performance and job satisfaction for most employees. However, the employer does not have complete freedom to make decisions in the personnel area and, even in areas where they have authority, they are often influenced by forces outside of the immediate program environment. The organizational, social, legal, and economic forces which govern various aspects of work life have increased markedly in number and kind in the last few years. Many day care programs have had difficulty staying aware of the responsibilities they assume as employers. They have even greater difficulty explaining to staff policies which are adopted of their own free choice versus policies adopted to conform to existing laws or regulations.

The actions of an employer toward employees is influenced by the type of organization sponsoring the day care program, policies of funding and regulatory bodies, state and federal laws regarding employee management, and the general effect of social and economic forces on day care employment. An effective day care employer needs to be aware of these forces, alert to potential changes which will effect work life in the program, and able to explain the impact of these factors to community leaders and board members, as well as to employees.

Type of organization

Both for-profit and not-for-profit forms of organization have implications for employer/employee relations. For-profit organizations (sole proprietor, partnership, for-profit corporation) all have an obligation to allow owners to receive a reasonable return on the money they risk in starting the business and, at the same time, to use the resources of the organization to the best advantage of children and employees. Employees need to recognize that the pursuit of some profit is an appropriate and necessary objective in this situation and for-profit employers should be more open with staff when such financial considerations have been an influence on management or program decisions.

Not-for-profit organizations are sometimes compared mistakenly to for-profit organizations in this respect on the assumption that their leadership is not motivated by personal gain when making program decisions. Yet, in this sector there is a tendency to undervalue the needs of employees because voluntary organizations are so often designed to meet the needs of a disadvantaged clientele. Leaders who work hard to solicit donations are usually highly committed to see that the money is directed toward services. They try to serve as many children as possible and sometimes expect unusual sacrifices of their employees in achieving this end.

The size and overall mission of the organization can affect personnel practices. Many day care programs are operated by units of state or municipal government, by public schools, or by organizations which have broader responsibilities, such as hospitals, mental health centers or community action agencies. Day care programs depend on an intimate, highly cooperative set of relationships among employees and between the director and employees. However, the larger the organization, the more likely it is to use a personnel management system which, though highly equitable, may be quite impersonal or inflexible.

Problems can arise if the overall personnel management system cannot be adapted to accommodate the day care component. For example, in some programs day care salaries are lower than those for staff working in other components of the organization because these other components have specific and relatively generous sources of funds to pay salaries. The day care program, on the other hand, can only resort to raising parent fees or cutting other costs if their salaries are to become consistent within the overall organization. Sometimes the situation becomes further confused if the day care director concludes that salaries cannot be raised, but is instructed to do so because of a system-wide management decision. If the director then resists this decision, employees' morale may be damaged; but if the decision is accepted, other parts of the program's operation may suffer.

Funding and Regulatory Policies

A day care program has little control over the number of staff it must employ in relation to the number of children to be served. The staff to child ratio is regulated by the day care licensing standards of most states, and is further defined by the policies of most public funding agencies. It is understandable that public agencies concerned with protecting children and promoting their development would focus on this concept. A staff to child ratio exists in all day care programs, is easily measurable, and seems to be significant proof of the program's intent to safeguard the well-being of the children. Staff to child ratios have an overriding impact on the cost of day care and many believe an equally important relationship to the quality of care for children. The subject is likely to remain controversial for some time to come, since it pits beliefs about how to make child care affordable against efforts to protect and promote the development of children.

A major multi-year study with a primary focus on issues of staff to child ratio is being reported at the time of the writing of this publication. Preliminary information from the National Day Care Study suggests that the notion of "group size" must also be taken into consideration.[1] Overall, the study should encourage greater flexibility in the thinking of day care directors and regulatory administrators related to all aspects of staff to child ratios.

Another kind of policy problem sometimes occurs when the day care program has a contract to use public funds to serve children. Some state or federal contracting agencies require that, as a condition of funding, the contractor adopt personnel policies which are determined by the funding agency. There is a legitimate basis for this request to the degree that fund source needs assurance that all federal and state laws related to personnel (e.g., equal employment opportunity laws, wage and hour laws, etc.) are being obeyed by the day care program.

However, some fund sources exceed this boundary and require that a uniform set of personnel policies be adopted covering all aspects of the employer/employee relationship. This is a questionable action on the part of the funding source because uniformity of personnel policies among a diverse set of contracting day care programs is unnecessary and undesirable, and may violate the legal nature of most contractor-independent agent relationships. Despite these serious reservations, some day care programs will probably have to continue operating under personnel rules determined by an external authority. In this case, the employer should be careful to explain the constraint to staff. It is normal for employees to make occasional requests for changes or upgrading of various personnel policies. It is difficult for employees, just as much as it is for the employer, to accept that this area of management policy cannot be controlled by the program.

Personnel Laws

Among important external influences on employer/employee relations are the state and federal laws regulating personnel matters. These

---

[1] National Day Care Study, Abt Associates, Inc., 55 Wheeler Street, Cambridge, Massachusetts 02138.

laws protect the right of employees to receive fair wages, to labor in a safe and healthy environment, and to have personal security during periods of unemployment, work injury or retirement. In recent years, our country has adopted a national policy to end discrimination in all forms of employment practices and has taken steps to protect the interests of minority groups. Dedication to such goals is a source of pride in a democratic society. However, translating these beliefs into concrete, easily understood standards and applying them has proved to be an elusive task accompanied by much confusion and continuing conflict among highly esteemed values.

Day care directors sometimes feel bogged down in trying to comply with the various laws and regulations. They find that the required paper work reduces time they could be spending in personal interaction with staff. They wonder how to screen prospective job applicants for the important personal qualities necessary to do day care work and yet avoid asking questions which might be construed as discriminatory. They raise questions of whether it is better to dispute a questionable claim for unemployment insurance to save money for the program, or to give a previously useful employee the benefit of the doubt. Basically these directors want to speak out for their rights as employers, while still showing staff they believe in the principle that employees have rights too. This is a difficult position to maintain.

If the director criticizes or appeals a decision of one of the agencies which administers personnel laws, it may seem to employees that the director has a negative attitude about employee rights. Oftentimes, this is not true at all. The problem may be that a given policy seems too impersonal or costs so much that the entire program is endangered. Yet, again without clear communication to staff, the director's motives can easily be misunderstood.

In some cases, day care directors have become so concerned trying to comply with various personnel laws that they have been intimidated in their role of directing and leading staff. This reaction often stems from an incomplete understanding of the laws and alternative ways to comply with them. Several sections of this publication are designed to correct this knowledge gap and to make it possible for individual centers to further research their alternatives.

Economic and Social Issues

Economic and social concerns of the times have a direct impact on many personnel activities. The general trend toward civil rights has given job applicants courage to challenge employment decisions, and high unemployment levels of recent years have created the necessity to vigorously pursue every job opportunity. From the employer side, this has resulted in increased attention to documentation and more detailed employment procedures. Further challenges have come from employees who have appealed disciplinary or dismissal decisions. Participation in such grievance procedures has proved to be a new and unpleasant work experience for most directors, and they are frustrated by some procedures which seem too much weighted in favor of the employee.

A final influence on the character of employer/employee relations is the important question of money. The impact of staff to child ratios on cost has been mentioned. Another major issue is the minimum wage law. As of this writing, the Fair Labor Standards Act calls for a significant increase in the minimum wage level during each of the next three years. While many programs agree with this increase, directors see it as a delayed time bomb which will sooner or later result in the cutting back of staff or the closing of some day care programs.

Another consequence of the rise in minimum wage has been the relative narrowing of salary differences among experienced or highly trained workers and new employees. Up to now, most day care programs have tried to reward more skilled employees with higher starting salaries and/or yearly salary increases. But now the increases in minimum wage have become so sizable that no money is left over for other salary objectives. The net effect has been a freezing of increments among more experienced workers and a subsequent lowering of morale among many of these employees.

Some day care programs are beginning to martial forces to cope with this dramatic increase in cost. Several publicly funded programs already report success in getting state appropriations for this specific budget item. Leadership in the for-profit sector is concentrating on a change in the formula for child care income tax deductions so that more of the cost of day care is deductible. This would make it easier for parents to afford the probable increase in fees that will be needed to pay higher wages. Whatever the final outcome, the internal and external pressure to increase wages in day care in the next few years will have an enormous effect on all other aspects of employer/employee relationships.

CHAPTER 2
Laws Relating to Personnel Matters

A prerequisite to a well-designed and implemented plan of personnel management is a thorough knowledge of laws which regulate various aspects of employment. This is no small chore, since there are several laws and their application varies depending on the legal form of organization under which a day care program operates. The situation is further complicated by the fact that there are many different interpretations of the laws and their enforcement. There is considerable difference from state to state and, sometimes, various interpretations among inspectors in the same office. It should be remembered that some of these major laws have been in existence for a very short period. Confusion, and perhaps even overreaction, accompany most social changes; we are still in that period.

Because of this, a day care program trying to understand all its legal responsibilities can be caught in dilemma. Programs have been known to contact a federal or state agency to inquire about the applicability of a particular law to their situation, only to find out that their question had never been asked before. The agency, with very little appreciation of the specific nature of day care, might make an interpretation consistent with how the law applies to some large industrial setting. The day care program finds itself having to choose between fighting a very large inflexible public enforcement body or accepting a questionable ruling which may add unnecessary cost in time or money. More than one day care program has asked itself whether it would not have been better to remain blissfully ignorant just a little bit longer.

This is not to suggest that programs should evade laws or regulations with which they disagree, but serves as a reminder that the day care program has the right to question interpretations of the law and implementing regulations; to ask that the opinion of more than one local level enforcement person be used in making a judgment; and to find out whether the same law is being given a similar interpretation in other communities.

Before reviewing the list of personnel-related laws which apply to day care, it should be noted that information on this subject is likely to become outdated relatively quickly. New laws, amendments to existing laws, and administrative rulings could change the circumstances related to a particular day care program. Therefore, the reader should consider this information as a general guide, correct at the time of writing, and as a basis to begin an inquiry into the current situation. It should also be recognized that the material in this chapter will focus on establishing a factual understanding of each law. While some interpretation or discussions of implications will be offered, the majority of comments will be reserved for other chapters when application of the law is related to specific personnel issues.

Civil Rights Act of 1964— Title VII

(As amended by Equal Employment Opportunity Act of 1972)

1. **Level of Government:** Federal
2. **Definition of Employer:** *All* private employers of 15 or more persons, all educational institutions (public and private), state, local and federal governments.
3. **Basic Provisions:** Prohibits discrimination because of race, color, religion, sex, or national origin in any term, condition or privilege of employment. This applies both to applicants for jobs and employees.
4. **Responsibilities of Employer:** The employer must remove "artificial, arbitrary and unnecessary barriers to employment" in practices and

7

policies of recruitment, selection, placement, testing, systems of transfer, promotion, seniority, lines of progression, and other basic terms and conditions of employment. *All* employers must post a notice about the filing of charges. Private employers of 100 or more must file an annual report (EEO-1) on racial, national origin, and sex composition of their work force by occupational category.

5. **Source of Further Information:** U.S. Equal Employment Opportunity Commission, 2401 E Street, N.W., Washington, D.C. 20506. Request the publication: *Affirmative Action and Equal Employment—A Guidebook for Employers, Volumes I & II.*

The Equal Pay Act of 1963
(as amended)

1. **Definition of Employer:** All employers subject to the Fair Labor Standards Act.
2. **Basic Provisions:** Employer must provide equal pay for men and women performing similar work. Coverage extends both to hourly employees and executive, administrative, and professional employees.
3. **Source of Further Information:** U.S. Equal Employment Opportunity Commission, 2401 E Street, N.W., Washington, D.C. 20506.

The Age Discrimination in Employment Act of 1967
(As amended by the Age Discrimination in Employment Act of 1978)

1. **Level of Government:** Federal
2. **Definition of Employer:** Employers of 25 or more persons.
3. **Basic Provisions:** Prohibits discrimination against persons age 40-70 in any area of employment.
4. **Source of Further Information:** U.S. Department of Labor, Employment Standards Administration, Wage and Hour Division, Washington, D.C. 20210.

Executive Orders 11246 and 11375

1. **Level of Government:** Federal
2. **Definition of Employer:** Federal contractors and subcontractors.

3. **Basic Provisions:** Requires an Affirmative Action Program by all federal contractors and subcontractors with a contract of $10,000 or more. The term "contract" does not include "grants" but it is advisable for employers with federal "grants" to comply also.
4. **Responsibilities of Employer:** Must file an annual report (FED-1). Firms with contracts over $50,000 and 50 or more employees must develop and implement a written program.
5. **Source of Further Information:** Employment Standards Administration, Office of Federal Contract Compliance Program, Third and Constitution Avenues, N.W., Washington, D.C. 20210.

Rehabilitation Act of 1973—Section 503

1. **Level of Government:** Federal
2. **Definition of Employer:** Federal contractors and subcontractors.
3. **Basic Provisions:** Prohibits job discrimination because of a handicap and requires affirmative action to employ and advance in employment qualified handicapped workers. Any contractor of $2,500 or more must comply.
4. **Source of Further Information:** Employment Standards Administration, Office of Federal Contract Compliance Program, Third and Constitution Avenues, N.W., Washington, D.C. 20210.

Vietnam Era Veterans' Readjustment Assistance Act of 1974—Section 402

1. **Level of Government:** Federal
2. **Definition of Employer:** Federal contractors and subcontractors.
3. **Basic Provisions:** Prohibits job discrimination and requires affirmative action to employ and advance in employment:
   (1) qualified Vietnam era veterans during the first four years after discharge;
   (2) qualified disabled veterans throughout their working life if they have a 30 percent or more disability.
4. **Source of Further Information:** Employment Standards Administration, Office of Federal Contract Compliance Program, Third and Constitution Avenues, N.W., Washington, D.C. 20210.

Department of Treasury— Internal Revenue Service Ruling

(Published in Federal Register, **Volume 46, #233, Tuesday, November 18, 1975)**

1. **Level of Government:** Federal
2. **Definition of Employer:** Private schools applying for tax exemption under section 501(c)(3) of the Internal Revenue Code of 1954.
3. **Basic Provisions:** A school that wants to qualify as an organization exempt from federal income tax must have a nondiscriminatory policy as to students. A school must show affirmatively that it has adopted a racially nondiscriminatory policy as to students, that this is made known to the general public and that since the adoption of that policy it has operated in a bona fide manner in accordance with this policy.
4. **Responsibilities of Employer:** Record keeping requirements include, among other things, records indicating the racial composition of student body, faculty and administrative staff.

State and Municipal Laws

Comment: Many states and municipalities have passed laws related to employment discrimination.

Wage and Working Condition Legislation

The Fair Labor Standards Act of 1938

(As amended by the Education Amendments of 1972)

1. **Level of Government:** Federal
2. **Definition of Employer:** All employers of enterprises having workers engaged in interstate commerce. Some employees of state or local government may not be covered by the wage and overtime provisions. All preschools whether public or private or whether operated for profit or not. (Any establishment which has as its only employee members of the owner's immediate family is not covered by the act.)
3. **Basic Provisions:** Establishes a minimum wage, equal pay, overtime pay, record keeping requirements and child labor standards. Bona

fide executive, administrative or professional employees are exempt from the minimum wage and hour provisions of the act.

It does *not* require: (1) vacations, holidays, service or sick pay; (2) a discharge notice or reason for discharge; (3) rest periods, holidays off or vacation; (4) premium pay holiday work; (5) pay raises or fringe benefits; (6) a limit on hours of work for employees 16 years of age or older.

Minimum wage rate is:
Beginning 1/1/79 — $2.90/hour
1/1/80 — $3.10/hour
1/1/81 — $3.35/hour

4. **Responsibilities of Employer:** Employers are required to keep records on wages, hours and other items. Employers must display a poster which outlines the Act's requirements. Punishment for violation of FLSA may be in the form of a fine not to exceed $10,000 for the first offense or a fine and a prison term not to exceed six months for a second violation. A two-year statute of limitations applies to wage suits involving non-willful violators; three years is the period for willful violation.
5. **Source of Further Information:** U.S. Department of Labor, Employment Standards Administration, Office of Federal Contract Compliance Program, Third and Constitution Avenues, N.W., Washington, D.C. 20210.

State Minimum Wage Laws

Comment: Most states have passed additional wage and hour legislation with unique provisions. Such legislation is usually administered by a state labor department or similar agency.

The Federal Wage Garnishment Law

(Title III of the Consumer Credit Protection Act)

1. **Level of Government:** Federal
2. **Definition of Employer:** All employers.
3. **Basic Provisions:** It sets restriction in the amount of an employee's earnings that may be deducted in any one week through garnishment proceedings and on discharge from employment by reason of garnishment. The law does not change most garnishment proceedings established by state law, nor does it annul or affect any provision of a state law that provides

greater restriction on garnishments than under federal law.

4. **Source of Further Information:** U.S. Department of Labor, Employment Standards Administration, Office of Federal Contract Compliance Program, Third and Constitution Avenues, N.W., Washington, D.C. 20210.

Employee Benefit and Insurance Legislation

Federal Unemployment Tax Act of 1939/The Social Security Act of 1935
(As amended)

Individual State Laws Related to Unemployment Insurance

1. **Level of Government:** Federal and State
2. **Definition of Employer:** A for-profit corporation which employs one or more workers for at least one day in each of 20 weeks in a calendar year or who has a payroll of $1,500 in a calendar quarter must participate in the federal and state program.

   A nonprofit corporation which employs four or more workers 2 weeks in the current or preceding calendar year does not participate in the federal program but must participate in most state programs. Employees of churches, associations of churches or schools other than institutions of higher learning are not covered.

   Employees of state or local government may or may not be covered depending on state legislation.
3. **Basic Provisions:** Provides benefits (the amount varies depending on individual state laws) to unemployed individuals provided that claimants have a bona fide attachment to the labor force (established by the amount of wages earned in or number of weeks worked in the year preceding the initial claim) and that claimants be able to work, available for work and make a reasonable effort to find suitable work.
4. **Source of Further Information:** The state agency appointed to administer this law is usually the Department of Labor or Employment Security.

Social Security (Social Security Act of 1935 and Federal Insurance Contributions Act)

1. **Level of Government:** Federal
2. **Definition of Employer:** Employers who are units of federal, state or local government may choose to participate or not. All private for-profit corporations must participate. A self-employed individual must participate. (This would include a sole proprietor day care service.) A not-for-profit corporation may choose to participate or not.
3. **Basic Provisions:** Provides retirement, disability, burial and survivor benefits to eligible employees and self-employed individuals.
4. **Source of Further Information:** United States Social Security Administration, 6401 Security Boulevard, Baltimore, Maryland 21235.

Workman's Compensation

1. **Level of Government:** State
2. **Definition of Employer:** Varies from state to state.
3. **Basic Provisions:** Workman's Compensation Laws have developed on a state-by-state basis so it is difficult to provide information which applies uniformly. The typical law has three features: a) The basic operating principle is that an employee is automatically entitled to certain benefits whenever he suffers a personal injury by accident arising out of and in the course of employment. b) Negligence and fault are largely immaterial, both in the sense that the employee's negligence does not lessen his rights and in the sense that the employer's complete freedom from fault does not lessen his liability. c) Coverage is limited to persons having the status of employee, as distinguished from independent contractors. d) Benefits to the employee include cash-wage benefits, usually around one-half to two-thirds of his average weekly wage plus hospital and medical expenses. In death cases, benefits for dependents are provided; arbitrary maximum and minimum limits are ordinarily imposed. e) The employees and their dependents, in exchange for these modest but assured benefits, give up their common-law right to sue the employer for damage for any injury covered by the Act. f) The right to sue those persons whose negligence

caused the injury remains, however, with the proceeds usually being applied first to reimbursement of the employer for the compensation outlay, the balance (or most of it) going to the employee.

4. **Responsibilities of the Employer:** The employer is required to secure workman's compensation insurance through private business, self-insurance or, in some states, a state-operated program.

5. **Source of Further Information:** In most states the state insurance agency is responsible for monitoring private insurance plans and/or operating the state-funded insurance plan.

Employee Retirement and Income Security Act of 1974 (E.R.I.S.A.)

1. **Level of Government:** Federal

2. **Definition of Employer:** Private plans administered by an employer, an employee organization or both are covered.

   Governmental plans, church plans that do not elect coverage, and certain other exceptions are exempted from inclusion.

3. **Basic Provisions:** The law is designed to regulate (1) employer welfare benefit plans and (2) to regulate employee pension plans.

   (1) A welfare benefit plan is defined as "any plan, fund or program" established for the purpose of providing medical, surgical, or hospital care or benefits, or benefits in the event of sickness, accident, disability, death or unemployment.

   (2) A pension benefit plan is defined as "any plan, fund or program" that (a) provides retirement income to employee or (b) results in a deferral of income to employees for periods extending to the termination of covered employment or beyond.

   Note: By administrative regulation unfunded welfare plans and certain insured welfare plans which cover fewer than 100 participants are exempted from some of the reporting and disclosure requirements for welfare plans. This should include most day care programs because they have fewer than 100 employees. All pension benefit plans are subject to the reporting and disclosure requirements, however.

4. **Responsibilities of Employer:** In general the law (a) requires a series of reporting and disclosure of activities (b) establishes standards for the conduct of a plan administrator (fiduci-

ary) (c) establishes appeal requirements for employees denied benefits (d) establishes standards for guaranteed participation in benefit programs after a certain length of service and attained age (e) establishes standards for vesting of benefits (f) establishes standards related to the funding of plans and (g) provides a protection of pension benefits when business failure or merger results in the termination of a plan.

5. **Source of Further Information:** U.S. Department of Labor, Labor Management Services Administration, Office of Employee Benefits. Room S4516, 200 Constitution Avenue, N.W., Washington, D.C. 20216. In addition, some responsibilities are assigned to the Internal Revenue Service and Pension Benefit Guarantee Corporation.

Employee Health and Safety

Occupational Safety and Health Act of 1970 (OSHA)

1. **Level of Government:** Federal

2. **Definition of Employer:** Any for-profit or not-for-profit organization in any business affecting commerce. State and municipal government agencies are required to participate if their state has an approved plan for carrying out the provision of the act.

3. **Basic Provisions:** Requires that employers shall furnish employment and a place of employment free from recognizable hazards that could cause death or serious harm. Requires that employees comply with all standards issued under the act that apply to his own actions and conduct on the job. Key OSHA standards that apply to day care settings relate to drinking water, exits and exit signs, fire doors, fire protection procedures, lighting, lunchrooms, medical services and first aid, railings, stairs, storage, toilets, trash and wash facilities.

4. **Responsibilities of Employer:** Any private employer with 7 or more full- or part-time employees during the previous calendar year must keep records. They include (OSHA #100) a record of any recordable employee accident, a supplementary report (OSHA #101—or an appropriate substitute form) which must be filed within 6 working days after learning of an employee accident, and (OSHA #102) a summary

report which must be completed at the end of each calendar year. These records must be maintained at each work place and do not need to be forwarded to OSHA unless specifically requested.

5. **Source of Further Information:** U.S. Department of Labor, Occupational Safety and Health Administration. Room S-2315, 200 Constitution Avenue, N.W., Washington, D.C. 20216.

Information can be obtained in *General Industry—OSHA Safety and Health Standards Digest,* available from U.S. Government Printing Office, Washington, D.C. Publication #029-016-00027-5, Price $1.05.

Income Tax Withholding

Federal Income Tax

1. **Level of Government:** Federal
2. **Definition of Employer:** All employers.

3. **Basic Provisions:** To serve as the agent of the federal government in the collection of employee income taxes.

4. **Responsibilities of Employer:** Responsibilities include withholding tax and depositing it in federal depository bank, furnishing each employee copies of Form W-2 "Wage and Tax Statement" for himself and each taxing jurisdiction, and furnishing a copy of Form W-2 to the Internal Revenue Service.

It should be noted that failure to forward tax money to the U.S. government is a criminal offense. The party or parties responsible, whether a day care program director, owner of a for-profit program or Board member of a not-for-profit program, can be criminally prosecuted.

State or Municipal Income Tax

Comment: Many states and municipal units of government also require that the employer serve as their agent in the withholding of income taxes.

CHAPTER 3
Developing Written Policies and Procedures

A basic component of effective personnel management is to offer a clear set of policies and directives upon which employees can base their work. This facet of personnel management is usually conveyed through a series of written documents, the most important of which are: a) statements of goals and objectives, b) operations manuals, c) personnel policies and procedures manuals, d) parent policy handbooks, and e) job descriptions. These written documents are useful for parents and communities too, but for employees they are especially important.

A goal statement makes explicit those beliefs about the nature of day care and the needs of children which are embodied in the way the program is to be run. An operations manual defines how day-to-day activities will be handled; personnel policies state how employee problems will be treated and how benefits will be provided. Overall, well thought-out and clearly written policy and procedure documents help decrease supervisory problems, since they lessen the amount of misunderstanding over job responsibilities or disagreements about the rights and privileges of employment.

Day care programs vary considerably in the degree to which they have developed written policy and procedure statements. In small programs, where the director or owner is present each day, conversations are frequent and this may lessen the need for written instructions. Pragmatically speaking, there is great leeway in deciding which documents ought to be developed and how much time to spend in the process. Furthermore, because day care programs differ in their forms of organization and program philosophies, the actual content of policy and procedure documents will differ greatly. In this chapter and the accompanying appendices, a fairly detailed analysis of what subjects could be in each document is included. It is possible that some suggestions will not apply in individual cases but the information should provide a useful base of comparison from which a plan for a particular program could be devised.

Statement of Goals and Objectives

All day care programs are built on a number of important beliefs about what day care is, what parents need from a day care program, what children need to develop effectively, how day care fits into the concerns of a particular community, and how the type of organization which operates the program (for-profit or not-for-profit corporation, charitable group, government agency, industry, etc.) can best make day care available. As important as these concepts are, it is unusual to find a day care program which has crystalized its beliefs into a written statement. There are several reasons for this common omission. A goal statement is idealistic and abstract; it is sometimes difficult to see how it will have a practical use. Founders of day care organizations feel little need for a written statement of goals because they are so intimately involved in the program's establishment. Another common belief is that the goals of an organization will be self-evident once it begins to operate, so it is better to concentrate on getting the program in operation rather than in writing goals.

There is another side to this issue, however. The belief that founders of a program know its goals is often very true. But, this is less true of employees, especially those who are hired after the program begins. Even board members who join the organization after its establishment need help in identifying which values are most important. Goals are not always self-evident from a day care program's actions. In fact, once the action begins, the real possibility of conflict among various goals becomes evident.

While goals are usually broadly stated notions, they should be translated into concrete and more narrowly stated objectives. This action makes it possible to measure progress and gives a basis for public accountability on goals of one's own choosing rather than just those of various funding sources.

Lastly, outside events may require the program to change its goals from time to time. When a program has a written set of goals which is out of date, and another set of goals that is implied or verbally stated, confusion among employees results.

The sample of Goals and Objectives included in Appendix A is an abbreviated version of a set developed by SREB during a previous project which involved the establishment of day care programs for the purpose of demonstration and training in eight separate states. While the selection of goals includes the very individualized experience of deciding which values are most important to the organization, the sample can be useful in identifying overall topics for consideration. It is particularly helpful as a model of refining goals into a measurable form of objectives.

Parent Policy Handbook

As its name states, the Parent Policy Handbook is meant to be used by parents. However, it should be mentioned in a chapter on documents of value to employees because it is sometimes the primary source of information related to specific aspects of the parent-employee relationship. Topics, such as how fees are collected, what will be done if a parent is late picking up a child and whether a sick child will be accepted, have implications for employees as well as parents. Overall, the parent policy handbook contains the promises the program makes to parents related to care of the children and what kind of performance they can expect from staff. To reach maximum achievement, employees must know what these promises are. An outline for a parent policy handbook is contained in Appendix B.

Operations Manual

For an employee to do his job well, he must have an extensive amount of information describing the daily activities of the organization, how these activities are planned and executed, how to perform work which requires the cooperation of other employees, where to get information or a decision, what the specific duties of his particular job are, and what the standards of the organization are in determining good work performance. Most day

care programs have taken reasonable steps to supply this information to employees. Often it is in the form of memoranda on bulletin boards, a resource file for teaching staff, carefully written job descriptions or, in some cases, an operations manual.

An operations manual is a tool to centralize and systematically inform employees concerning all policies that relate to how work is to be conducted. Frequently, an operations manual includes step-by-step procedures on how particularly complex policies are to be carried out. Thus, a good operations manual supports the supervisory process by offering guidance and instruction, even when the day care director is not available. For example, the manual should discuss eating routines and instructions to insure that learning opportunities are promoted during meal time, that children are encouraged to at least try foods they do not like, that procedures for hand washing and teeth brushing are an automatic part of the daily procedure, etc. Similarly, the manual should include policies and procedures handling child discipline, health and fire emergencies, use of building and equipment, and the many other activities that staff must carry out if the program is to run well.

Operations manuals are often updated by the issuance of memos on specific topics. It is important to be systematic about this process. For example, sometimes a new policy is formulated and posted for staff to read. Soon the bulletin board gets crowded, the memo is removed and all traces of the new policy in writing *and* in practice disappear. A more practical approach is to develop the operations manual in loose leaf form. Each new policy is added in the appropriate place, and a policy which is no longer in force is removed. This technique insures that new employees know what is expected of them, and there is a clearer sense for all staff of how policy is made and how staff can influence management decisions when appropriate.

An outline for topics that could be included in a typical operations manual is included in Appendix C.

Personnel Policies and Procedures

Personnel policies and procedures may be part of the operations manual or may be a separate document. There are reasons for considering them separately.

The operations manual covers administrative areas over which the director has considerable discretion. That is, if a policy needs to be modified, the director usually has full authority to make that decision. However, personnel policies are often more formal statements and are changed less easily. Personnel policies describe the rights of employers and employees in the work relationship. They cover such areas as working conditions (hours, paydays, etc.), type of employee status (permanent, temporary, probationary, etc.), the salary and benefit structure, attendance and leave procedures, employee evaluation standards, types of disciplinary action and methods of appeal. Usually the director can make changes in these areas only in consultation with the board of directors or the owner. Separating the operations manual from personnel policies and procedures helps clarify this distinction. When developed as a separate document, it is possible to provide each employee a copy of the personnel policies and procedures—an advisable practice.

The content of personnel policies and procedures tailored to an individual day care program will vary depending on the form of the organization and the financial health of the program. A review of several sets of personnel policies currently used by for-profit or not-for-profit programs shows that they all suffer from lack of an overall statement about the worth of employees to the organization. This is important because the tone of the document can easily become negative. It is hard to write about grievance procedures and reasons for dismissal without sounding like an authoritarian employer. Another area which needs general improvement is the topic of disciplinary actions. Many personnel policy statements do not offer specific descriptions of those employee actions that might lead to suspension or dismissal.

Policies of leave and benefits vary the most widely. This is primarily attributable to economics. Some day care programs can offer only minimal opportunities for vacation, sick leave, or fringe benefits. Others can afford to be more liberal and provide choices which allow employees to suit their individual needs. Some of the most effective policies make a clear division between statements which are *policy* and statements which are *procedures to implement a policy*. In some cases, the manual points out which policies are mandated by federal or state laws. Such statements are included to inform staff about those policies which can be changed by the decision of the employer alone and those policies which are outside of the control of the employer.

Appendix D contains an outline of subjects which could be included in a statement of personnel policies and procedures.

Job Description

A job description is a concise and, at the same time, complete statement defining the duties and responsibilities of a particular position, the lines of authority to the position, and the qualifications, salary, and promotional opportunities of the position. A job description looks at the nature of the individual worker and is usually used to evaluate work performance. For this reason, it is advisable to give each employee a copy of his/her own job description.

At the same time, job descriptions are useful to the day care program as a whole. Job descriptions form the basis for newspaper advertisements to fill vacant positions; they are used by personnel committees as guidelines when interviewing job candidates; taken collectively, they form a composite statement insuring that all tasks needed to run the center are assigned, and that a system for fair salaries and career advancement is in place.

It is a common reaction for day care centers to revise their job descriptions after having been exposed to workshops on personnel management by increasing the amount and description of job responsibilities. Day care directors report that staff sometimes resent taking on duties which are not clearly spelled out to them during the hiring process and that thorough job descriptions are a safeguard to prevent such conflicts.

Another reason for revision of job descriptions is a growing awareness among day care observers of questions of legal liability. A recent book by Will Aikman, *Day Care Legal Handbook*[1] lays a solid basis for understanding most questions of legal liability which face a director, owner, board, or employees. In this context, it points out that employees "engaged in the business of the organization and acting within the scope of their authority" are not likely to be personally liable for an action they may have taken while working for the program. The job description provides documentation of that fact. Further discussion of the content of job descriptions and the process for their development is contained in Chapter 4. An example of a set of job descriptions is included in Appendix E.

---

[1]Available from Day Care and Child Development Council of America, Inc., 805 15th Street, N.W., Washington, D.C. 20005.

CHAPTER 4
Salary Plan

A salary plan is an attempt to establish salaries in a systematic way with attention given to levels of pay in the community and the relative worth of each job within the center. A salary plan is designed to be fair and consistent in its treatment of employees and is built on a classification of jobs that shows the degree of difficulty and responsibility of various kinds of work which employees do.

Many day care programs do not have a salary plan that meets the criteria mentioned above. In some cases, salaries are pulled out of the air at the time of hiring or are the product of negotiation between the director and the prospective employee. In other cases, salaries become the beginning salary to which has been added over a period of years a series of increases of varying size and at varying intervals of time. Thus, while the salary may reflect the value of long service and individual efficiency, there is not a clear sense of the actual worth of the job nor is there any consistency that other employees can count on in anticipating future salary potential.

Some programs stand by their current approach to salary management, arguing that this is an area where the employer should retain maximum flexibility; they can pay higher starting salaries to an unusually qualified applicant, or can use increments as regularly or infrequently as necessary to reward effective employees and provide incentive to less effective ones. Other programs point out that a long-term plan is really needed; that when the program started no one was really sure the program would survive and so a full scale salary plan was not developed. They have since had the painful experience of seeing some of their most effective employees leave for a higher paying job elsewhere.

Obviously, the availability of funds is an essential element in any effort to revise base salaries or increments in day care. As previously mentioned, increases in minimum wage rates will monopolize most, if not all, available monies during the next few years. However, that is not reason enough to avoid development of a program-wide salary plan. The increase in minimum wage is in itself a form of revision in the salary plan of most day care programs. But questions remain of whether it can be done in a way that is comprehensive in relation to all jobs in the program and whether the program can form a plan which includes its own goals and beliefs about compensation rather than one exclusively controlled by external influences.

Steps in Developing a Salary Plan
1) Describe and Analyze Existing Jobs.

The first area to explore is the current assignments of tasks and whether these are the most logical and efficient patterns to get overall work of the program done. This is accomplished through a process called task analysis. This simply means that all employees, or a sample of employees representing every job in the program, are asked to review their jobs and make an exhaustive list of tasks they are required to perform.

It helps to ask how frequently tasks are performed (i.e., daily, weekly, monthly, etc.), since employees might otherwise neglect to describe tasks which require considerable knowledge or skill but are not performed often. Other information to be gathered should include in what ways and how often immediate supervisors oversee the job; whether the employee supervises other employees; whether there are any safety risks in this work; and whether there are any specific qualifications to perform the work (e.g., ability to operate a typewriter, drivers license, etc.). The survey should also ask the employees' opinions of how much formal education and experience are required to perform their jobs.

When the comprehensive list is available, the director and/or personnel committee can review it to see whether some tasks should be combined into new jobs or whether some employees have been assigned responsibilities which the current system does not formally recognize. A number of possible decisions will occur at this phase.

It may be that the assignment of some duties will be changed. For example, a program may conclude that teacher aide jobs have generally involved no responsibility for planning lessons but that aides should handle some of this responsibility. Thus, a new duty would be added to that job. In another case, the issue might be the combining of duties from two previous positions into one job with expanded responsibility. For example, day care programs often combine part-time positions of janitor and bus driver into one full-time position. In some cases the study of tasks results in the establishment of new positions. For example, one day care center discovered that teachers reported a considerable amount of time was used in assignment to another classroom when a teacher was sick or on other leave. The center created an additional position called a "roving teacher." The roving teacher does all substitute work and on other days is assigned to children needing individualized attention.

2) Develop Job Descriptions.

Once the duties of each job have been reaffirmed or changed, a set of job descriptions should be developed. The job description is a summarized version of the information gathered in the task analysis. It contains information about the necessary qualifications and responsibilities of the job and will be used in weighing economic importance. Based on experiences in many industries and research on employee opinions of what factors give worth to a job, most employers weigh the following factors:

Nature of the work itself. How important this job is to completion of the center's goals, the relative difficulty, variety and complexity of the work, and whether the work is a recognized profession or technical field.

Degree of responsibility. Whether the job involves much independent action versus one which is routine, or are there available guidelines in the form of policies, procedures, or standard practices.

Responsibility for supervision of others. This includes relative size and complexity of the operation

supervised, and subordinate supervisors or direct service staff.

Nature of supervision received. This includes the extent to which and purpose for which work is reviewed by others.

Degree of contact with public. The amount of contact involved and the degree of discretion allowed in interpretation are important variables.

Special working conditions. Whether the job involves unusual, unattractive, or unsafe working conditions.

Knowledge, skill or ability required. This includes the nature and relative difficulty of the knowledge or skills involved and the ability to operate specialized equipment.

Training and experience required. This includes the level of general education, level of specialized or professional education and the nature or length of experience required.

3) Classify the Job.

When each job has been reviewed and its important characteristics described, it is time to classify each position in relation to other jobs. This is a process designed to group jobs of similar difficulty into the same class regardless of how dissimilar their functions may be. Each class is then ranked in the order of importance to the program.

To start, identify jobs with similar responsibilities, for example, all with teaching duties. At this point some programs will decide that there is only one level of responsibility involved in the teaching task, while other programs will conclude that there are two or three levels (e.g., lead teachers, teachers and teacher aides). Next, compare these jobs having similar functions with other jobs in the program. For example, some programs argue that any job which works directly with children requires more knowledge and skill than the work of a cook. Other programs argue that a correct analysis of the cook's job indicates a wider variety of skill, knowledge, and responsibility than is required in most aide-level teaching jobs. Whatever conclusion a particular program may reach, it should be based on the objective information contained in the job description.

At this point each job has been placed in a "class" with jobs of similar difficulty. For most day care organizations, only six or seven classes will include all possible jobs. The classification approach helps to simplify decisions about salary since it can now be assumed that each job in a given class has the same dollar value as every other job in that class.

The second major phase in classification is to determine the relative importance of each class of jobs to the overall operation of the day care program.

A simple technique for helping to think through a job classification is to develop a chart which shows the classification visually (see Figure 1). Jobs in the same class would be shown horizontally and the ranking of classes would be shown vertically.

Figure 1

Class 1			Center Director	
Class 2		Head Teacher		
Class 3			Bookkeeper	
Class 4	Cook	Teacher		
Class 5				Custodian
Class 6	Assistant Cook	Teacher Aide	Clerk/Typist	Bus Driver

4) Conduct a Pay Survey.

The first step in determining how much to pay for a given job is to find out how much money other employers are paying for similar work. This step introduces a note of reality into a process which is otherwise subjective, and gives a clear impression of how much will have to be paid if salaries are to remain competitive and good employees retained.

The process for conducting a pay survey is relatively simple and can yield some of the most important data gathered. The program should contact day care employers representing the for-profit, not-for-profit, and government-operated sectors. A request should be made for information about job classes and base salaries in each of these programs. It is also advisable to seek information from employers outside of the day care field. For example, secretarial and bookkeeping skills are used by many different kinds of employers. Even with a more day care oriented skill, such as teaching, the program should attempt to contact a variety of employers who have needs for similar skills. In the latter example, salaries for teacher aides in a school system or workers in programs for exceptional children should be compared with the day care program's salary scale.

Some day care directors report difficulty in gaining salary information from other employers. This is understandable since many employers consider the question of salary levels to be highly personal; some fear that revealing such information will lead to attempts to recruit staff away through offers of higher pay, and others believe that withholding this information is a prerogative based on principles of private enterprise and maintaining competitive advantage.

While difficulties may arise, it is important to persevere in gathering comparative salary data. It is often the quality and range of information secured in this step which insures the credibility and acceptance of the pay plan. Eventually employees and board members will review the proposal and comment on its fairness and overall soundness. For both groups, a wide-ranging pay survey is one of the most concrete pieces of evidence available and is frequently a major factor in resolving final questions.

5) Consider Relative Value of Fringe Benefit Options.

The pay survey as well as the job classifications should lead to a tentative figure for the base rate of pay for each job. However, a second factor to consider is the value of fringe benefits offered. Fringe benefits will be discussed more fully in the next chapter. At this point what should be realized is that fringe benefit plans vary considerably and their worth to a given employee varies depending on individual circumstances. In some programs the fringe benefits available to an employee may be quite generous and involve substantial employer investment. If this is the case, employees may have a strong incentive to continue in employment and a lesser need for higher salaries. In other cases, the fringe benefits may be minimal and the employees may prefer additional fringe benefits in lieu of higher salaries. In other cases, employees may feel that increased salaries take precedence over any form of fringe benefit. No matter what the circumstances, the relationship between available or desired benefits and salaries should be reviewed before a new pay plan is instituted.

6) Determine Salary Range and Increment Policies.

The steps taken so far are useful for establishing the basic dollar value of the job and particularly the starting salary that most employees will receive. However, to be fully useful, the pay plan must provide a framework for deciding the questions of when and for what reasons salary increases should be given. There is no one pattern of increment policies which can be recommended for every day care program. However, dissatisfaction over salary increment decisions is a common concern among employees in all types of organizations. To a great degree, this concern usually centers around the fairness of a given decision and the clarity of explanation for the decision. For these reasons, an employer should carefully examine the logic behind any increment related policy, knowing full well that sooner or later it will have to be justified to staff. There are four common reasons for granting increments:

Qualifications

The beginning salary is a measure of what should be paid to a job applicant who meets the minimum level of education and/or experience called for in the job description. Sometimes applicants demonstrate an unusually advanced level of education and/or experience, in which case, it is assumed that these applicants will make a contribution to the organization more quickly and with less time spent in initial training and supervision than candidates who meet only the minimum requirements. Thus, it may be justifiable to pay such applicants higher starting salaries since their worth to the program is greater. Furthermore, highly qualified candidates are likely to have potential worth to other employers too, and so the employer must be willing to compete financially in order to gain their services.

A similar situation occurs when staff add to their educational qualifications (e.g., earn a vocational certificate, a Child Development Associate certificate, or a college degree). Again, the advanced knowledge and skill are assumed to improve work performance to the point that the employees' worth increases materially.

Employers who want to build this factor into the pay plan do so by establishing for each position a beginning salary plus several steps of increase. These steps are usually percentage increases. For example, the second step may be 5 percent more than the first step, the third step 5 percent more than the second, and so on. While a salary range allows leeway to appoint the highly qualified candidate to a higher level, it can be designed so that there is self limitation in the process to insure fairness to the rest of the employees. This is done by including a policy that limits the maximum number of steps above basic level (usually two steps) which will be offered to applicants no matter how qualified they are.

Merit

Most increases are based on the belief that if employees are performing well, they deserve financial rewards. Such "merit" raises are an incentive to continued good performance and encourage employees to improve performance. Conversely, if employees are not performing well, they should be denied increases until their work improves. In its

purest form, an employer who adopts this approach would give raises as often as a particular employee had shown an especially noteworthy achievement, and the size of the raise would vary in proportion to the value of the employee's contribution. Furthermore, this approach assumes that some marginally effective employees would rarely, if ever, get raises, and that extremely effective workers would be rewarded often and generously.

This approach to raises developed in private industry and is often practiced in for-profit day care programs. Its principal benefit is its influence on employee motivation and retention. Many day care directors or owners report that this is positive. However, in its pure form, it is an approach about which employees may frequently have questions. Employees who do not receive raises are likely to become dissatisfied without strong guidance as to what they must do in the future to reach satisfactory performance. Furthermore, the system can become unwieldy when each employee is paid at a different rate. The longer the system operates, the more difficult it is for the employer to weigh various factors determining a specific decision's fairness compared to past decisions. This makes employees, sometimes even the ones who benefited most, feel that decisions are too subjective. In some cases this approach is accompanied by a belief that discussion of salaries is a personal matter between the employer and the individual employee and should not be disclosed to other staff. While there is certainly a basis for such a belief, it restricts employees as a whole from getting information which would allow comparisons, and thus heightens speculation that the salary structure is subjective or unfair.

Length of Service

This is an approach which is a variation on the "merit" theme but has some distinct characteristics. The length of service theory argues that the worth of employees doing the same job will increase as they gain skill and knowledge in their work experience through the years, and this increased effectiveness should be rewarded. In this approach there is an assumption that the period of increase should be predictable (e.g., once a year) and that the increase is likely to apply to most if not all employees, rather than only the most outstanding. Further justification for this approach lies in the notion that having many long-term employees decreases employee turnover, thus freeing management from recruiting, interviewing, and training new staff.

Employers who adopt this theory use a system of salary ranges with each step a percentage apart. They examine the work record of each employee regularly but, except in rare cases of poor work performance, they increase all employees one step each year.

Most length of service approaches place a limit to the number of steps assigned to each job. For example, teacher aides may be eligible for length of service increases during each of the first five years of employment, but after the fifth year they cannot earn any further raises based only on length of service. This policy assumes that there is a limit to how much knowledge and skill can be gained in one job. In addition, it serves as an incentive for employees to aspire to more responsible and more skilled work. Thus teacher aides who are at the end of the salary range recognize that further salary increases can only come if they become teachers, a job which is more difficult and which, therefore, has a higher base salary.

Cost of Living

Because the length of service approach increased the salary of employees every year, it was often considered to assure that salaries maintained pace with the cost of living. For example, if a salary step was 5 percent and the cost of living for that same year was 5 percent, then purchasing power of the salary increase allowed the worker to keep pace with the increase in the cost of living. In the example cited, employees did not get the theoretical reward for additional skill and knowledge earned, but were able merely to continue to buy the same goods and services as when first hired. This contradiction in the purposes of length of service raises has existed for some time without resulting in total dissatisfaction by employers or employees. However, in recent years, the cost of living has risen at a higher rate (10 percent to 12 percent per year) than the rate upon which most day care salary systems are built (5 percent to 7 percent per year). Some employers have acknowledged this fact and, when funds were available, have instituted an adjustment in the entire salary system to account for "cost of living" increases. However, confusion occurs when em-

ployees expect both a cost of living increase and a length of service raise in the same year. This aggravates the argument about the purpose of length of service raises and is becoming more and more financially unmanageable. Although it is too soon to tell, what may result is a tendency to eliminate "length of service" raises and substitute "cost of living" raises on a more regular basis.

Implement the Salary Plan and Review Regularly

The results of the previous steps should create a systematic salary plan. Hopefully, it will be a plan which gains employee confidence and which simplifies performance of this basic management responsibility. Actual implementation of the plan should probably be assigned to one individual (either the day care program director or owner) since no matter how carefully the salary plan is structured, determination of pay for each employee involves some subjective judgment. If desirable, the implementation phase can include a "check and balance" process in the form of an advisory committee of staff or board who can review the decisions. Such a committee should be composed of people who have perspectives balancing both program and employee needs.

Involvement of supervisors in salary decision is an important question. Particularly in plans with merit increments, the immediate supervisors' knowledge and judgment about employee performance is needed. However, it is important to train supervisors to make rational and fair judgments about employees and to gain an appreciation of salary questions from a program-wide perspective.

Finally, a salary plan should be updated. While the process to establish a plan may not need to be repeated for several years, the structure should make it possible to review specific areas as needed and to adapt to changing circumstances.

CHAPTER 5
Employee Benefit Programs

Employee benefits serve to provide income to employees other than in the form of salary. Some employee benefits or fringe benefits are mandated by law, while others are voluntary. Some fringe benefits are paid for entirely by the employer, while others are financed jointly by the employer and the employee. Employee benefit plans recognize that in a complex society the economic and personal welfare of employees is a shared concern involving government, employer, and employee.

The variety and breadth of coverage of various employee benefit options has grown steadily in the last several decades. Some estimates indicate that by the mid-1980s employee benefit forms of compensation may amount to $50 for every $100 spent on wages and salaries directly.[1]

Most day care programs report that they are unable to offer employee benefit programs which are as generous as those available through other human service organizations, let alone what industries offer their workers. Obviously, the economics of the field have been the determining factor in this decision. Yet it is important to have an understanding of employee benefit programs. Knowing the rationale for such programs, their influence on staff, and alternatives to financing makes it possible for day care organizations to gain maximum benefit from legally mandated programs and to seek out voluntary opportunities which can be reasonable in cost compared to the rewards the employer and employee receive.

There are several different values to an employee benefit program:

Security. Certain benefits establish the workers' personal security against hazards associated with work, such as medical payments for work-related injuries, disability pay for workers who become temporarily or permanently disabled, and support payments during periods of unemployment. Non-work crises are equally important. Many employers offer health, hospitalization, and life insurance. Retirement is another significant concern which is addressed both by Social Security legislation and many private pension plans.

It should be recognized that the desirability of such benefits is very much affected by the age and individual circumstances of employees. Research has shown that younger workers desire more base salary while older workers seek security.[2] Thus, day care program directors who tend to be older than staff may place a higher value on such benefits than the employees themselves. On the other hand, many employees are not well-educated concerning the need for various income assurance programs; it should be the responsibility of the employer to provide information on this subject. One study, for example, found that of people aged 35 to 64, 97 percent believed in early planning for retirement, but only 28 percent were actually doing anything about it.[3] Thus, the employer may need to establish a program even before the staff recognize its value.

Efficiency, Cost Savings and Convenience. In many instances employee benefits provide services that employees intend to buy and would do so using their direct salary. However, they prefer to work through the employer. The range of alternatives available in the field of health, life, and retirement insurance is quite complex. Often the employees want help in selecting the program or programs which are most desirable. They are willing to share some of this decision with an employer who is able to study the options and receive professional advice before selecting a limited number

---

[1] Deidrick F. Willers, *Federal Regulation and the Employment Practices of Colleges and Universities,* The Regulation of Employee Benefit Programs on Campus, (National Association of College and University Business Officers).

[2] Jay R. Shuster, "The Trouble with Employee Benefit Programs," *Business Management,* Volume 39, Number 6, (March, 1971), pp. 34-37.

[3] Patricia L. Kasschaw, "Revolutionizing the Need for Retirement Preparation Programs," *Industrial Gerontology,* Volume 1, Number 1, (Winter, 1974), pp. 42-59.

of choices to present to staff. Frequently, the employer-sponsored benefit plan is less expensive, since it can be secured at a group rate. This is an important rationale in day care where salaries are otherwise low. Furthermore, most employees recognize the convenience involved in having the employer assist in completing forms, processing claims and deducting the employee's share of costs directly from their paychecks.

Tax Relief. Some benefits have the effect of increasing the services available to an employee without increasing his taxable income or, at least, tax payments can be deferred to a future year. For example, if an employer pays $100 per year toward the cost of life insurance, the employee does not have to pay income tax on this amount. However, if the employer increases the employee's wages by $100, the employee would have to pay income tax on that $100. This particular advantage may be less compelling in many day care settings since the lower the initial salary, the less the tax savings that can occur.

Mandatory Benefit Programs

By far, the major portion of money spent on employee benefits by day care organizations is devoted to complying with mandated benefits (i.e., Social Security, Unemployment Insurance, and Workman's Compensation). In recent years there has been a trend for day care directors or owners to feel an adversary relationship with the various mandated programs. As Social Security rates increase, as more claims are experienced and rates increase under Unemployment and Workman's Compensation, day care employers have become more adamant in asserting their rights in using hearing and appeal procedures. However, day care employers must recognize that such programs meet the principal security needs of staff. If there are frustrations with the current structure, employers should work toward constructive reform, but they must help staff understand that criticism of the existing system is not an effort to undermine their individual security.

Social Security
Old Age, Survivors, Disability and Health Insurance (OASDHI).

The Social Security Act establishes programs related to many areas of human welfare, including unemployment insurance and aid to families with dependent children. However, the portion of the act of most universal interest relates to Old Age,

Survivors, Disability and Health Insurance.

Financing. The OASDHI provision is financed by a joint contribution of employer and employee and/or by the contribution of a self-employed individual. The 1979 OASDHI contribution rate (F.I.C.A.) is 12.26 percent on the first $22,900 of each employee's earnings 6.13 percent contributed by the employer and 6.13 percent contributed by the employee. The rate for a self-employed person is 8.1 percent. Both the wage base and the contribution rate are scheduled to increase in the future, with the latter reaching 14.30 percent (7.15 percent each) by 1986.

Eligibility. An employee is eligible for Social Security benefits after gaining credit for work measured in quarters. A quarter is any three-month consecutive period of a calendar year in which a person is paid a minimum of $50 in wages for work covered by Social Security. A worker and certain members of his or her family can receive some monthly retirement benefits at age 62, and monthly disability benefits at any age if he or she is "fully insured." A retiring worker currently needs between 22 and 40 quarters of credits to be fully insured. A disabled worker must have from 6 to 40 quarters of credits to be fully insured, depending on age at the time of disability. "Currently insured" is a term applied to special coverage for those who die before becoming fully insured. To qualify, a person must have at least one and one-half years of work within three years before his or her death.

Retirement Benefits. The amount of pension a person receives depends upon his or her average monthly wage in covered employment. In calculating the average, up to five years of lowest or no earnings may be dropped. Social Security offices have charts available which show the amount of monthly pension available at different average annual earnings.

Survivors' Benefits. If a worker dies, monthly survivors' checks may go to certain members of his or her family, and a lump-sum payment of up to $255 in burial expenses may also be made, generally to the widow or widower.

Disability Benefits. Benefits are payable for medically determinable physical or mental impairments "which can be expected to result in death or which can be expected to last for a continuous period of not less than 12 months." The amount received is the same as the disabled worker would be allowed if he or she were 65 and had applied for retirement benefits. Dependents of disabled workers are also entitled to benefits.

Medicare Programs. In 1966, by amendment to the Social Security Act, the Congress established two health insurance programs for persons age 65 and over. Part A: Hospital insurance covers up to 90 days of hospital care for each spell of illness. Part

B: Supplemental medical insurance covers physician's services, home health services (without a requirement of prior hospitalization), certain medical services in addition to those provided in Part A, outside the hospital treatment, and hospital diagnostic services. Part A of medicare is free. Part B must be purchased and employees should be encouraged to sign up for it. To have full protection, the employee and or dependent spouse must sign up for Part B in the three-month period prior to either's 65th birthday.

OASDHI and Not-for-Profit Organizations

While the employers and employees in private for-profit organizations must participate in OASDHI, Congress had originally intended that units of government and not-for-profit organizations who had been declared tax exempt by the Internal Revenue Service should not have to participate. At a later time, Congress amended the law so that units of government and tax exempt organizations could join if they chose to do so. This is a decision which has proved confusing and controversial within the day care field; the facts are as follows. When a not-for-profit organization is first established and has gained *federal tax exempt status,* it may choose whether or not to join OASDHI. If it chooses not to join, neither employer or employee would be required to make the F.I.C.A. contribution. However, the employee should know that in this case they will not be earning quarters toward their eligibility. If the not-for-profit employer chooses to join OASDHI, then an election must be held to allow individual employees to choose whether they individually wish to participate. Any employee who chooses not to join will not have a F.I.C.A. contribution withheld, and the employer is not obligated to contribute. All employees who are hired after the election, however, must automatically participate in the program.

The not-for-profit organization may also choose to withdraw from OASDHI. This process is somewhat more complex. It requires that the Social Security Administration be notified two years in advance and renotified one year before withdrawal.

Unemployment Insurance

Unemployment insurance is a federal-state cooperative program which provides a weekly income for a limited period of time to compensate workers who are unemployed through no fault of their own. The Federal Unemployment Tax Act

(FUTA) sets forth certain minimal provisions to which the individual states must conform. Beyond these basic standards, the states have considerable flexibility in tailoring programs to meet their own needs. No two states administer programs and determine benefit levels and eligibility in identical ways, though all have basic similarities. For unemployment insurance purposes, a commercial "employer" is a person or organization employing one or more workers in each of 20 days in a year, each day being in a different week, or with an annual payroll of $1,500 or more.

Eligibility. The federal unemployment insurance law does not, for the most part, control eligibility and disqualification, as states are generally free to establish their own rules and regulations. The test for eligibility is threefold: the employee must be able and available to work; must be free from disqualification (due to such acts as quitting voluntarily without good cause or separation due to misconduct); and must not refuse suitable employment. The net effect of this test is to eliminate unemployment insurance payments to those workers who are not employed primarily because of noneconomic causes. In addition to this basic eligibility test, all states require an unemployment insurance claimant to have earned a specified amount of wages in order to qualify for receipt of benefits.

The federal law also recognizes three conditions under which a claimant may refuse to accept a job. These are: (1) if the job is available due to a labor dispute; (2) if the wages or conditions of employment are substantially lower than area standards; and (3) if as a condition of taking the job, the employee would be forced to join a company union or refrain from joining a labor organization.

Rates and Taxes. Several factors are used to determine the rate of contribution to the unemployment insurance fund by an individual employer. This is further influenced by whether the employer is a for-profit or not-for-profit organization. While the subject is complicated, most day care organizations try to understand these factors, recognizing that a lower expenditure in this category would free funds for other purposes.

Voluntary Benefit Programs

The limitation of resources, as well as pressure from staff to use available funds for direct salaries, has resulted in a restricted number of voluntary benefits being available in the majority of day care programs. However, it is in this area that employers can be most creative. Through investigation and planning they can seek to offer as wide a range of options as possible and secure the greatest benefits for the least cost. Voluntary benefit programs can offer plans which supplement mandated benefits or can focus on additional personal needs of employees and their families. The typical voluntary benefit program covers four areas.

Leave and Supplemental Pay

Time off with pay for vacation, holidays, or during an illness are commonly available benefits which are not required by law. Some day care programs extend their paid leave programs for certain civic responsibilities including serving on a jury, serving as an election officer, or serving on military duty. The number of days allowed for sick leave and vacation is often determined by the number of years of employment, thus rewarding longer-term employees (i.e., an employee with one year's experience gets one week paid vacation, while an employee with three years gets two weeks paid vacation, etc.). However, some centers follow a rationale that direct that work with children is demanding and those engaged in that work need extra time for rest and rejuvenation. In these centers, staff who work directly with children are given more vacation time than administrative staff.

Many day care employees would like to have leave time to take additional training. This is a desirable benefit since it helps both employers and employees. Educational leave may be granted either with or without pay at an employer's discretion. In the latter case, however, both employer and employee should formally recognize that the leave is voluntary. Otherwise, the Fair Labor Standards Act might be used to require that wages be paid for time spent in training.

Insurance[4]
Health Insurance

Programs of insurance for health and hospitalization, such as the Blue Cross and Blue Shield Plan, are almost a necessity and about 9 out of 10 persons in the United States under the age of 65 are covered by private health insurance; chiefly group insurance plans connected with employment.[5]

In general, health insurance includes three kinds of coverage: hospital, surgical and medical, and major medical. Sometimes these are in three separate policies and sometimes they are com-

bined. Hospital coverage usually includes: room and board, inpatient charges (for prescriptions, drugs, X-rays, laboratory fees, etc.), ambulance charges, emergency room care for accidental injuries, and specified maternity care. Surgical and medical coverage usually includes: payment for specified surgical procedures performed in a hospital or doctor's office, the services of an anesthesiologist, in-hospital physician visits and, in some cases, laboratory and X-ray fees. Major medical coverage is designed to pick up where hospital and surgical insurance leaves off. That is, these policies cover the cost of medical expenses in excess of limits usually included in basic health insurance plans. Major medical helps insure against a "catastrophic" illness which might otherwise exhaust a family's savings and assets. Such plans define which expenses will be paid for, establish a maximum benefit level, and usually require that the insured pay a certain amount before the coverage begins.

Life Insurance

Life insurance protects an employee's family against loss of income in the event of the wage earner's death. Life insurance can be purchased as permanent insurance which has a cash value or term insurance which has no cash value. Many policies contain special provisions insuring against accidental death of the employee or covering the lives of spouse or dependent children.

Income Disability Insurance

Income disability plans are designed to supplement the disability provisions of social security by insuring periods of short term disability and by providing additional benefits beyond those provided by Social Security.

Retirement Plans

Retirement plans seem to be less available in day care than most other forms of voluntary benefits. Cost is a major inhibitor, but to some degree the youthfulness of staff and the uncertainty of long-term survival for many day care programs are other factors. Until recently, most day care employers and employees felt great confidence in the retirement provisions of the Social Security Act. Now, however, the prevailing opinion asserts that the federal program offers little more than the bare

---

[4] Portions of this section were taken from *Working Draft of Insurance Information for Child Care Personnel* by Professional Pensions, Inc., May, 1976. Mimeographed paper prepared for the D.C.C.D.C.A., 805 — 15th Street, Washington, D.C. 20005.

[5] Donald M. Landy, "Negotiated Health Plans," *Monthly Labor Review,* Volume 92, Number 5, (May, 1969), pp. 3-10.

minimum necessary for survival. Concern for a more comfortable standard of living after retirement will likely produce pressure for day care employers to supplement Social Security with a private retirement program. The recently passed federal law regulating retirement programs E.R.I.S.A. (see Chapter 2) should help day care programs who are about to initiate a retirement program. It helps employees by guaranteeing entitlement to benefits after a certain period of years of employment and by insuring that private programs will not go bankrupt. It also helps small employers by spelling out their responsibilities and those of the organization from whom the retirement program is being purchased.

There are four kinds of pension plans. All can be purchased from insurance companies, banks, or mutual funds companies. The four types of plans are described briefly in this section to indicate general information which may be of importance. For a more detailed description and discussion of advantages or disadvantages of each approach, a day care program should consult an accountant, lawyer, or pension plan representative.

Regular Pension Plan

This type of plan is available for employees of not-for-profit corporations, for-profit corporations, and the employees of partnerships or self-employed businesses. The plan usually includes provisions requiring a waiting period and a minimum age before an employee can join. There is also a "vesting" period, at the end of which the employee owns the employer contributions in trust or has a vested right in them. The vesting period can be immediate or up to 10 or even 15 years. The employer contributes to the pension plan based on an agreed-upon percentage of the employee's salary. Most plans allow employees to make additional contributions to the plan if they wish.

Keogh Plan

A Keogh Plan is available to partners or self-employed persons and their employees. This type of plan allows participants to contribute up to 15 percent of earned income per year (up to a maximum of $7,500). This money is not taxed until it is received. Benefits from the plan are not available until the age of 59 1/2 and must be taken by age 70 1/2. If a participant chooses to withdraw from the plan prior to the period of benefit eligibility (i.e., before age 59 1/2), a penalty is charged against the interest earned on the money.

Individual Retirement Annuity (IRA)

IRA is available to all persons with earned income who do not participate in a retirement plan. In this approach, participants can contribute up to $1,500 per year and the money will not be taxed until it is received. Again, benefits are not available until age 59 1/2 and must be taken by age 70 1/2 and an interest penalty is charged for early withdrawal of contribution.

Tax Deferred Annuity

This form of retirement plan is available only to employees of not-for-profit corporations which have received federal tax exempt status. This approach allows employers and/or employees to contribute up to about 20 percent of salary into the plan. The employee contribution can be deducted from taxable income for federal income tax and, in some states, can be deducted from state income tax. When an employee leaves employment, contributions are available as an "annuity" or as a cash settlement.

Services and Privileges

There are many specific goods or services employers can offer to raise employees' standard of living, enhance their feeling of worth to the organization, or create a more pleasant atmosphere for work relationships. In the larger, more affluent business world the range of options includes paid moving expenses, company cars, membership in private clubs or other benefits. The day care world may need to set its sights a little lower, but employers can be inventive. For example, many day care employers allow children of the employees to attend the day care center free or at a reduced rate; some programs provide assistance in securing or paying for employees' state-required medical exams; some pay fees for staff to participate in conferences and professional groups; others provide financial assistance to staff who wish to attend college courses. On a more personal level, some day care programs make it a point to take employees to lunch on their birthday; others allow staff to have time off to attend parent-teacher conferences regarding their own children.

Many centers offer payroll deduction plans for purchasing U.S. Savings Bonds. A service less commonly available, but of great overall value, is participation in an employee credit union. Credit unions pay relatively high rates of interest on employee savings while providing loans at relatively low interest rates. To establish a credit union usually requires a minimum of 50 employees or more. However, it is sometimes possible to join a credit union of another employer who has the required number of employees.

Another strength of day care programs which may be tapped for the benefit of employees is their regular contact with health, social service, and educational agencies. The established contact is usually directed to the individual needs of an enrolled child or family or the training needs of staff. However, it might be productive to discuss with these same agencies services or voluntary education opportunities which might be made available for employees. Having a thorough knowledge of the many resources in a community is a skill that most day care programs take pride in acquiring. A further challenge is to discover ways this infomation can be used to support employees and their families.

CHAPTER 6
Selection of Staff*

The importance of capable employees is underscored throughout this publication, thus the significance of an effective plan for hiring staff should be self-evident.

The hiring process can involve hours of work writing newspaper ads, answering phone calls, explaining how to fill out job application forms, and interviewing a large number of people just to fill one position. Sometimes directors feel that an inordinate amount of time is spent on this duty and that overall supervision of the program suffers every time a position is vacant. On the other hand, they recognize that selection of an applicant who proves to be an unsatisfactory employee is equally disruptive to the smooth operation of the program and that even more time may be required to straighten out problems.

Another concern comes from directors who recognize the fallibility of both themselves and any brief process used in determining which applicant will actually prove to be an effective employee. They point out that a small amount of written material and an interview of only 30 or 45 minutes can be misleading. Some people who would have made steady and valued employees may not present themselves well during the job interview while other verbally-skilled applicants appear to be excellent but do not work out once hired.

In recent years a third concern has centered around the need to build in procedures which guard against intentional and unintentional discrimination. Day care program directors are not sure how widely a job must be advertised, what questions can be asked on the employment application or during the interview, what documentation is required to prove that all candidates are treated fairly, and so on.

Purpose

There is more than one objective to a good hiring plan. Obviously, finding the most qualified employee is the paramount task. Yet, beyond determining which applicant is more capable, the employer should be interested in presenting the center as a good place to work. This requires honesty, not just image building. It is a step which will attract desirable applicants to choose the organization over other available job opportunities and it indicates that, even at the level of pre-employment discussions, the employer has an interest in the kind of communication which maintains good employee relations.

The terms and conditions of employment should be discussed, and an employer should be careful not to make promises related to salary, benefits, hours, etc., that cannot be kept. Similarly, the selection process can be used to identify training or supervisory needs of the person who is hired. A well-functioning employment process does not discover perfect employees, but does indicate strengths and limitations and offers some projections of the applicant's potential to grow. The employer should, therefore, use the employment process to define what information, skills, or attitudes will require attention during the first months of employment.

Finally, the action of notifying the community that a vacancy exists and of discussing the job opening with a variety of candidates and references is a ready-made opportunity to publicize the program. As the importance of the specific job is explained, the importance of the program to children and to the whole community is being explained also. Day care directors have commented that job applicants are frequently the source of information about community resources or donated materials that could help the program. Furthermore, the speed and courtesy with which job inquiries and other communication to applicants are handled will be noticed and remarked upon by a whole array of community people familiar with various applicants.

*The general outline and specific sections of this chapter are based on "Staff Selection: Choosing the One from the Many" by Roger Neugebauer, Printed in *Child Care Information Exchange*. For further information write: Child Care Information Exchange, 70 Oakley Road, Belmont, Massachusetts 02178.

Planning An Effective Selection Process

An ideal selection process should:

- Successfully notify several qualified applicants that a position is vacant.
- Use the employer's time efficiently and take advantage of strengths in the organization (board members, parents, staff) who can contribute to effective selection.
- Give the employer sufficient information to judge how the knowledge, experience, skill and values of each candidate will affect potential as an employee.

Recruiting

In most communities the announcement of a job opening, particularly for an entry level position, will produce large numbers of applicants. This could prove to be more of a hindrance than an advantage if the applicants have only modest potential to be employed. To increase the number of appropriate applications, the center should focus on recruitment sources that know the nature of day care work and the kinds of people who perform well in a day care setting. Some of the best sources of recruitment include: employees and friends of the program who refer applicants; applications submitted voluntarily based on the day care program's reputation in the community; training institutions with strong early childhood programs; local professional organizations; and notices in local child care newsletters.[1] In newspaper advertisements describing the position carefully will screen out applicants for whom the salary is too low, the education or experience requirements are too high, or who would find the challenges of day care work unsatisfactory. The employer should also be aware of recruitment obligations incurred through equal employment opportunity legislation. These are mentioned later in this chapter.

Efficient and Effective Procedures
Selecting Reviewers.

One area in which rethinking of the employment process may be useful is the question of who will be involved in various phases (interviewing, etc.) and how they will be used. Approaches to this question are quite varied. In some small programs, where the owner and director are one and the same, the tendency is to reserve most of the responsibility for employment activities for the director. The rationale for this approach rests with the belief that good employees are so critical that this area must be handled by top management only. Many not-for-profit organizations have a board personnel committee which shares hiring responsibility with the director or, in a few cases, takes full responsibility. Although board members have ultimate responsibility for the organization, in general, it is advisable for a board to exercise their hiring power only in relation to the director. That is, the board may be involved in the selection of staff, but they should allow the director the final decision. Some programs involve parents in a consultative role when making employment decisions believing that parents have so much at stake that the program has an obligation to seek their opinion.

Having additional people help in different phases of employee selection can contribute to the depth and variety of techniques used in reviewing candidates. When two or three people are available to help, it may be possible to interview all candidates rather than eliminate some on the basis of job applications alone. Having more than one person interview applicants or having one person interview and another person observe applicants in teaching situations can contribute to insight and objectivity.

Using other employees to assist in the selection process is an approach that is widely used and which appeals to most directors. The main argument for this involvement is that staff who have duties similar to those of the position to be filled can help identify in very specific terms the strengths and limitations of applicants to perform that job. There is also conviction that, since day care staff must work in close cooperation, using staff members helps to identify candidates most likely to fit into the program's team. It is also widely believed that the person who directly supervises employees, whether it be a cook, lead teacher or whomever, should have a say in which employees are selected.

A few day care program directors have reported skepticism with the idea of using employees to help select staff. They recognize that involving staff in such a key decision would contribute to the democratic leadership style that most staff prefer but they feel that it could also undermine this very process if the director did not agree with the opinions of staff. They also point out that vacancies offer opportunities to seek employees with particular skills or interests that might compensate for known weaknesses in the program. Yet, staff do not always fully accept criticism about the program's strong and weak points and the employee selection process is clearly the wrong forum for resolving this kind of question. In any event, programs that are considering involving two or more

---

[1] Neugebauer, p. 5.

people in aspects of employee selection should know that it has much potential, but it must be well thought through; each participant must be trained to perform his/her particular role, and the degree to which each participant's input will be used in making a final decision must be understood in advance.

Gathering and Assessing Information

Most selection procedures in day care settings include five steps: resume or application review, preinterview screening, employment interview, observation in a work setting, and reference check. The function of each of these steps is to gather information which, taken as a whole, will provide a complete picture of applicants' capacity to work effectively in the job under consideration. The success of the process depends on the employer's knowledge of what information should be gathered, a plan for insuring that most of the information is gathered through these five steps and, to some degree, on the skill or imagination of the employer in gathering some of the more complex kinds of evaluative information. Sometimes after a pattern for completing these five steps has been developed (e.g., employment application form designed, letter requesting references standardized, etc.), a program loses some of its focus on why certain information is requested and how it should be used. Thus, it is important from time to time to review these five steps and ask basic questions about them.

Knowledge, Skill, and Values

The three most important things an employer should know about applicants are whether they have the knowledge, skills, and values to work effectively.

Knowledge is the most concrete area. Does a teacher's aide candidate know anything about child development theory, methods of teaching, and techniques for handling difficult children? Does an applicant for the cook position know nutrition theory, techniques for bulk purchases and storage of food?

Skill is a more abstract concept and, therefore, more difficult to assess. Skill includes both the capacity to apply knowledge effectively and abilities acquired through observation or practice. For example, can a recent graduate from a college or technical school actually use "textbook" expertise? How well does a particular teacher candidate lead children in storytelling, science experiences, etc.?

Values are the most controversial information area. Sometimes they can be determined easily and sometimes only with great difficulty. Usually, they are a major factor in determining which candidate is finally hired. Values describes a point of view about something, a set of feelings about the subject, and a willingness to place that topic in relation to other important topics. Value issues include: What is the candidate's attitude toward work in general? Will the candidate be satisfied with the salary, working conditions, and nature of the work? What are the applicant's values about children? About organized child development experiences? About parents who place their children in day care?

Each of the five steps in employee selection can be used to determine some aspect of knowledge, skill and values and a variety of techniques have been devised to bring this information out. Some of these approaches will be described in the next section. However, the overriding point is to determine what areas of knowledge, skill, and values a program needs to know and develop a plan which successfully gathers this information from each candidate.

The Selection Process
Review of Resumes or Job Application Forms

A review of a resume or job application form helps to evaluate candidates' previous job experience and level of academic achievement. Generally, a form developed by the program is better because it will provide information on what the center needs to know. A resume could be misleading if information which might be judged unfavorably is left out or if the importance of previous work activities is exaggerated. It is during the review stage that applicants without basic job requirements can be screened out. For example, if a state licensing regulation requires that employees be at least 18 years old, candidates younger than that would have to be eliminated. Or, if the program has a policy that lead teachers must have a college degree in child development, then candidates without that background would be eliminated.

Preinterview Screening

To narrow a long list of applicants prior to a lengthy employment interview, programs screen by phone; others prefer a brief personal screening interview. The preinterview screening should focus on an outline of the job describing duties, wage and benefits, hours of work, etc. If the employer has questions about information on the job application (e.g., experience, training, expectations, etc.), some specific questions could be asked. A preinterview process will screen out those applicants who are not interested in the job and those whose preparation or personality is clearly unsuited.

Employment Interview

Usually, the most important step in the selection process is the employment interview. The opportunity to meet candidates face to face and to explore in-depth their experiences and qualifications is a powerful tool for making employment decisions.

Interview Format

Interviews may last from 45 to 60 minutes with a break of about ten minutes in between interviews to give interviewers a chance to write down comments about previous applicants and review written information about the next person to be seen. To keep impressions fresh, some directors prefer to see all the candidates in the space of a day or two, even if there are a large number of applicants. Other directors prefer to see only about three applicants per day, believing that mental fatigue sets in if too many applicants are seen at any one time. However, an effort should be made to complete all interviews within a week's time.

Although most often there is only one interviewer, some programs involve two or three interviewers either meeting an applicant jointly or separately. Either strategy is designed to obtain more than one point of view about the applicants. However, for some applicants, interviewing before a group tends to further increase anxiety which is likely to be already high. Meeting two separate interviewers, on the other hand, can sometimes relax applicants. Questions or omissions in the first interview, usually come out in the second interview.

Setting the Atmosphere

Finding a job is a test of one's worth as an individual. It determines whether a person will have enough income to live comfortably and it requires that someone make a judgment comparing knowledge and personal traits against those of other people. It is no surprise then that most applicants are nervous and, in their desire to present the best view of themselves, they are hesitant to recognize their own limitations. It is important, therefore, to develop a setting and an interview style which will reduce anxiety and encourage applicants to speak freely and honestly. Applicants should be greeted immediately upon arrival, preferably in person or with a sign indicating that they are in the right place. When applicants are taken to the interview room, they should be introduced to the interviewer and seating arrangements should be informal.

Assessing the Applicant

There are several general kinds of information exchanged in the initial phase of the interview. Assuming that a preinterview screening has taken place, applicants should already be familiar with a general description of the job, salary, and working conditions, and some specifics about the day care program. However, this information will need to be summarized and any questions answered. Similarly, questions the interviewer may have about applicants' previous work or experience should be addressed. At this stage, interviewers have a tendency to talk too much. He/she seems to be giving out information, rather than gathering it. However, for those applicants who have never worked in day care, the particular job and the program in general must be described in sufficient detail so that they can envision what the job will be like. It is only after they have gained such insight that the interviewer can ask effective evaluative questions. On the other hand, if the position requires advanced training and experience, the interviewer should assume that applicants have a fair degree of basic knowledge about the nature of the work.

Probing the more in-depth areas of knowledge, skills, and values can best be done by developing in advance a series of broad questions to be asked of every candidate. Each of these questions should be followed by spontaneous questions triggered by the individual responses of candidates and designed to get clarification of their thinking. Questions designed to measure knowledge (e.g., What are good music activities for four-year-old children? What should a sample daily program look like?) can sometimes be answered in a "rote" or memorized fashion and do not really tell how well the applicants understand the subject.

Questions about skills and values can be asked most effectively through case examples. These are questions which describe a problem as it would occur in a day care program and allow the interviewer to judge feelings as well as the thinking ability of candidates faced with a similar situation. For example, How should a teacher handle two children fighting over a toy? What if a child became angry and kicked the teacher in the leg? How would a teacher respond to a parent who was upset because a child got dirty at the center? Questions like these do not always have a single right answer and they can make applicants feel uncomfortable. Yet, they can be of value to applicants if it gives them a chance to recognize difficult aspects of the job before any commitments are made. The interviewer can assist in making this phase of the interview as easy as possible by praising candidates for answering questions openly and thoroughly. While it is probably not wise for the interviewer to disagree with ideas of applicants, it may be necessary to explain a policy if it is different from the ideas expressed by various applicants.

A final phase of the interview involves a summarization. Applicants should be asked if they have any other questions about the job. It is also a good idea to ask applicants to state what were the most important points about the job or their ability to do the job that were brought out by the interview. A question of this nature often identifies one or more issues which applicants viewed differently from the interviewer and leads to a few clarifying questions or remarks. Finally, the interviewer should let the applicants know when the final selection will be made and how applicants will be notified of the results.

Observation in a Work Setting

Seeing teaching candidates in a classroom is a useful selection technique. It provides a direct means of assessing the candidates' relationship with children and staff and also measures reaction to the physical environment. Some programs do not use this approach and should be encouraged to take advantage of its potential. The limitations of the approach should also be recognized, however. An observation format involves additional time of applicants and the employer, and is sometimes difficult to schedule. It takes time for children to get used to a new person in the classroom. Furthermore, applicants should be instructed on the role they are expected to play (i.e., an observer, an activity leader, or just a participant). For these reasons, each observation requires preparation and may take several hours to complete. Some day care programs shorten the process by simply giving candidates a brief tour of the facilities and asking for comments on what has been observed. Other programs request that promising

applicants volunteer a full day in the program and then involve staff who worked with the candidates in discussing their observations.

Reference Check

A thorough and candid evaluation by someone who has known an applicant for an extended period is an excellent assessment tool. Characteristics of applicants' personality or work attitude can be identified through this process—dependability, initiative, adaptability, and leadership capacity. Yet, reference checks contain more potential pitfalls than other assessment steps and should be used with caution.

The most useful references come from people who know both the applicant and the day care program seeking the reference. The quality of such a judgment will be known to the program and this is an important factor in assessing the information.

Former employers are a primary source of references, but the usefulness of this source has decreased in recent years. Hesitancy to state negative aspects of a former employee's work has increased because of the possibility of a libel suit or a civil rights violation. In some cases, employers have adopted a policy of only verifying the dates of employment without giving further information.

Checking references in person or by telephone is the most effective means of soliciting detailed and candid information. References requested by letter are often returned slowly or not at all and usually contain only general information. Important questions to ask are the length and nature of the relationship between the candidate and the person providing the reference. Did this person directly supervise the candidate? Describe the qualification of the job and ask the person to comment on how well the applicant meets these qualifications. Just as in a job interview, response to the broad "qualifications" question should be followed up by further specific questions depending on information given by the person providing the reference. Finally, an attempt should be made to elicit a broad overall judgment. Questions should include: Why did the candidate leave? Would you hire the applicant again? Is there any reason you would not recommend this candidate?

Many day care programs request that applicants also provide personal references. This is sometimes helpful but also has limitations. Quite naturally, applicants select as references persons who view them positively. Sometimes such persons have only seen the positive side of the applicants' personality and are unaware of their deficiencies. At other times, these people have a personal attachment to an applicant and are reluctant to share a knowledge of the applicant's weaknesses out of a desire to help the applicant gain employment.

A final step in completing the reference process is to document this information for the day care program's personnel file. Information the reference person supplies which may affect whether the person should be employed or not should be summarized in writing. This serves as a protection to the day care program in those cases where an unsuccessful candidate challenges the selection process.

Deciding Whom to Hire

With all the information that has been collected, it would seem like a simple task to select the best applicant, but it is often not easy. Sometimes one applicant emerges who stands well above the rest. A brief review of other candidates exposes justifiable reasons why each should be eliminated in favor of this candidate. Yet, if the candidate's salary requirements or expectation for advancement are high, it may be that he or she will not remain satisfied in the job very long.

In other instances, the employer may feel disappointed that none of the applicants seems highly suitable. This feeling can be based in reality, i.e., no well-qualified applicant actually applied. Yet, this same letdown can evolve from the nature of the employment process itself. Employee selection tends to rekindle the employer's own enthusiasm for the importance of each and every job in the program. The repeated description of the value of day care work and the responsibilities of the job to be filled make the employer keenly aware of the "potential" good there is in every job. It is no wonder then that applicants who do not yet share that insight and enthusiasm do not measure up to the employer's standards. At the same time, the employer should remember that "potential" lies in applicants too. It is possible to help employees grow on the job. With the right kind of employer support, employees who were considered only fair prospects at the time of hiring, can grow to a level of excellence.

Another common outcome in employee selection is the dilemma of finding two or three leading candidates whose strengths and weaknesses seem about equal. Directors who have had to chose among candidates where the differences were narrow, report that the determining factor is usually a matter of values rather than knowledge or skill. A second key determinant in this situation is which candidate will best balance the skills or personal attributes of the existing group of employees.

Along with the all-important question of who will be selected, day care programs must address the notion of how the decision will be made. In the many cases where only the director or owner has been involved in the selection process, the final decision is a relatively straightforward activity. In those programs where several people have participated in interviewing or observing, the process must accommodate their contributions. As in other phases of employee selection, the input of several people widens the viewpoints and sharpens perceptions about each candidate.

When a group is involved, it may be possible to get a quick consensus in favor of one candidate. More likely, each candidate will need to be discussed and a gradual process of elimination will occur. Focusing on *all* of the qualifications required for the job tends to place in proper perspective those candidates who have one particularly positive or particularly negative characteristic. The final selection can come through a vote process although in most cases arriving at a consensus decision is a better approach. Voting can be quick and clear but sometimes leads to dissatisfaction among people who advocated for a losing candidate. The concensus method sometimes requires an extended discussion until all points of view have been aired but insures that the applicant selected will be supported by everyone concerned from that point on.

Employment Agreement and Other Follow-up Responsibilities

Once the selection has been made, the employer should give attention to arriving at an employment agreement which is fair to both parties and consistent with any discussion held during the selection phase. The candidate chosen should be notified as soon as possible by phone. This offer should be confirmed by letter stating the title of the position, the rate of pay, the starting date, the benefits, probationary requirements and, if appropriate, any other special conditions or promises that were agreed to. When the candidate accepts the position, all other applicants should be notified that the position has been filled.

Equal Employment Opportunity*

The application of equal employment opportunity laws as they relate to employee selection is a complicated subject which often leaves directors

---

*The basis for much of the information in this section is *Affirmative Action and Equal Employment, A Guidebook for Employers*, Vol I and II. Available from the U.S. Equal Employment Opportunity Commission, Washington, D.C. 20506.

confused and frustrated from trying to understand legal terms, references to court cases and information which appears to be conflicting. What follows is an attempt to summarize the most important aspects of equal employment laws as they relate to selection. In a general sense, it should help day care employers recognize that they are still relatively free to establish qualifications and ask most questions which are important in determining an applicant's ability to work in day care.

One note of caution should be stated about this section, however. As with other material in this publication related to personnel laws, it could become outdated due to changes in court interpretations or further amendments to the Civil Rights Act. This material can serve as a general guide, but it is advisable for day care programs to maintain contact with a representative of the Equal Employment Opportunity Commission, or a similar agency at the local level, to answer specific questions and to keep up with continuing developments.

The Civil Rights Act of 1964 Title VII is the major federal law designed to provide all persons an equal opportunity for employment regardless of race, religion, color, sex, or national origin. The Age Discrimination in Employment Act adds the same protection to people age 40 to 70. These laws represent an effort to eliminate past patterns of discrimination as well as to insure that all future employment will allow free and open access for all qualified applicants. The laws apply to all employers of 15 or more employees and, therefore, include most day care programs. As stated in Chapter 2, several other laws or regulations exist, but they have less general application since they only apply to organizations which have contracts or subcontracts with the federal government.

These laws and subsequent court interpretations recognize that, in general, employment discrimination is not the result of a deliberate malicious act on the part of one individual against another. Rather, it is often an inbred practice in an employment situation which does not single out any one individual but in a subtle or even imperceptible way can be discriminatory to a minority group as a whole. Thus, by definition, employment discrimination is a class-wide discrimination, and it is the *consequences* of an employment practice—not the *intent* which determines whether a particular practice will be declared discriminatory.

Recruitment

In the recruitment phase, it is important to recognize that relying on "word of mouth" or "walk-in" applicants alone tends to perpetuate the present composition of the work force. This practice has been declared discriminatory by the courts in cases where groups protected by the law were not well represented in the work force. Thus, while not absolutely required, it would be advisable to develop a recruitment process which includes public advertisement and, if appropriate, announcement of job openings through minority-based community groups. Furthermore, in newspaper advertisements the phrase "Equal Opportunity Employer" should be used, since this is publicly recognized as a statement of intent to comply with Title VII and other such legislation. Finally, for purposes of self-improvement and self-protection, it is advisable to keep a record identifying all persons who were interviewed and reasons why they were not hired.

Selection Criteria

The interview and selection process is known to be the point where most discrimination occurs and it is in these areas that it is most difficult to offer "yes" or "no" explanations of what should be done.

Congress or the courts have identified several areas where a potentially discriminatory piece of information can be gathered and used in making an employment decision. However, in each case, the permissible question has been very narrowly defined and employers have been cautioned that they will be expected to provide a thorough justification for their action should a discrimination charge be filed. The exceptions are as follows:

Religion

The 1972 Amendments of the Civil Rights Act created Section 702, which provides that Title VII shall not apply to a "religious corporation, association, educational institution or society with respect to the employment of individuals of a particular religion to perform work connected with the carrying on by such corporation, association, educational institution, or society of its activities." The basic effect of this section is to allow institutions *which claim that status* to give preference to employees of a particular religion.[1]

Section 702 may apply to day care programs which are operated by church organizations. However, it would be advisable to consult with the Equal Employment Opportunity Commission to be sure that a particular religious organization meets the requirements of this section. It should also be noted that where preferential hiring based on religion results in discrimination against one of the other protected groups in the act, it may still be unlawful.

[1] George P. Sape, "Title VII of the Civil Rights Act of 1964 as Amended." In *Federal Regulations and the Employment Practices of Colleges and Universities,* Washington, D.C.: National Association of College and University Business Officers, p. EEP-7.

"Bona Fide Occupational Qualification"

This is a phrase which recognizes that in certain rare cases, an employer may hire members of one sex exclusively. Such cases would be where there is a need for authenticity (e.g., model, actor, actress) or when the sexual characteristic of the employee is crucial to performance of the job (e.g., wet nurse). There does not seem to be an example of a "bona fide occupational qualification" involved in day care work, so this category probably does not apply.

"Business Necessity"

The courts have declared that a practice which has a "disparate effect" on groups protected by the law may be used if an employer can demonstrate compelling "business necessity" and that no alternative nondiscriminatory practice can achieve the required purposes. The courts have interpreted "business necessity" narrowly, requiring overriding evidence that a discriminatory practice is essential to safe and efficient operation of business and/or showing extreme adverse financial impact. Even so, the principle of "business necessity" is often referred to in helping an employer decide what qualifications can be established for a job and what questions can be asked to determine a particular applicant's qualifications.

It is the "business necessity" exemption which is most likely to have application in day care settings. Selection procedures subject to this policy include all tests, personal histories, biographical information, background requirements, specific educational or work experience requirements, interviews (scored or unscored), application forms, and interviewer rating systems.

The courts have not yet ruled on whether a number of specific questions can be asked in the pre-employment process particularly since the "business necessity" exemption would vary greatly depending on the type of business. However, in evaluating whether a question should be asked, it may help to consider these three questions: Does this question tend to have a disproportionate effect in screening out minorities and females? Is this information necessary to judge this individual's competence for performance of this particular job? Are there alternate, nondiscriminatory ways to secure necessary information? Keeping these points in mind, it may help to consider some of the questions day care programs may have an interest in asking.

1) Race, National Origin, Religion

Pre-employment inquiries about race, color, religion, or national origin, do not constitute per se violation of Title VII, but such inquiries or recording such information in personnel files will be examined carefully should discrimination charges arise. On the other hand, the employer may feel the need to keep such information if he desires to review current hiring practices for purposes of self-improvement or self-protection. The determining factor—for both employer and a potential compliance investigator—is the *effect* of record-keeping. If employment of minorities is adequate or increasing, an affirmative action purpose may be documented. If a discriminatory pattern remains, there is presumption that race and sex identification in a personnel file may contribute to the situation.

2) Education

Courts have found non-job-related educational requirements which have a disparate effect on protected groups are a type of illegal discrimination. Specifically, the requirement of a high school degree as a condition of employment or promotion where there is no evidence that it is a significant predictor of job performance has been prohibited.

3) Work Experience

In a large number of situations, a requirement of experience will be directly job-related and a legitimate measure of employee selection. However, as in many such valid requirements which do not have a discriminatory intent, the issue of validity under Title VII is somewhat more subtle. In an occupation which has historically been filled with all or predominately white, or all or predominately male workers, a requirement of prior work experience may perpetuate past discriminating acts.

4) Physical Requirements

Standards related to height, weight, and other physical requirements should be used only where necessary for performance of a particular job. Many day care programs feel strongly that applicants for teaching positions should be capable of lifting children in case of injury and sitting or kneeling on the floor in order to teach at the child's "eye level." These requirements would have to be justified on the basis of "business necessity."

In 1978, Congress passed an amendment to the Civil Rights Act which makes it illegal to refuse to hire a woman because she is pregnant.

5) Sex, Marital and Family Status

Whether a candidate is male or female, married or single, and number and age of children are examples of questions frequently used to discriminate against women, and which rarely relate to capacity in job performance. Again, such questions can be asked but, should a charge be filed, the employer would have to prove that the purpose for asking the question and that the actual use of this information was not discriminatory. It is a violation of the law for employers to require pre-employment information on child care arrangements from female applicants only. The Supreme Court has ruled that an employer must not have different hiring policies for men and women with preschool children.

6) Age/Date of Birth

This information can be gathered. However, since it could be used to discriminate on the basis of age, the employer would have to have a solid justification should a charge of discrimination be filed.

7) Arrest and Conviction Records

An individual's arrest record has been ruled by the court to be an unlawful basis for refusal to employ, unless a "business necessity" for such policy can be established. A federal court has also ruled that conviction of a felony or misdemeanor should not, by itself, constitute an absolute bar to employment, and that the employer should give fair consideration to the relationship between the nature of the act resulting in conviction and the applicant's fitness for the job in question.

Many state day care licensing laws or their implementing regulations include a provision which prohibits the hiring of a person convicted of child abuse or neglect. This particular requirement has not been challenged as a Civil Rights Act violation, and it is probable the "business necessity" exemption would apply so that a state agency or an individual employer could prohibit the hiring in day care of a person *convicted* of child abuse or neglect.

8) Transportation To and From Work

An employer may inquire whether an applicant has an adequate plan for transportation to and from work.

CHAPTER 7
Supervision

Supervision of staff is probably the most interesting aspect of day care personnel management, and probably the most critical to a successful day care program.

Based on facts and principles, supervision also requires imagination and creative leadership for both job productivity and job satisfaction of employees. At the same time, it requires realism. Working relationships in day care programs do not always flow smoothly; there are individuals or groups of employees who have grievances; there are employees whose work is unsatisfactory and sometimes employees whose poor performance requires dismissal.

William Van Dersal defines supervision as the "art of working with a group of people over whom authority is exercised in such a way as to achieve their greatest combined effectiveness in getting work done."[1] As this definition suggests, there are many areas of skill and knowledge involved in being a manager of work and a manager of people. Good supervisors must know how to guide and direct the efforts of the people they are responsible for, and take into account the many individual differences and needs of employees. They must be able to teach people how to perform existing jobs and prepare staff for positions of greater responsibility. Good supervisors must be able to design a plan of operation for their units, including being able to schedule work, determine priorities, and judge what is a fair day's work for each employee. Good supervisors must be concerned with their own self-development; they need to learn how to speak and write clearly; how to read and how to listen. Lastly, they must understand and support the needs of the organization they work for and contribute ideas and actions which help the organization grow in efficiency and quality.[2] This is an ambitious list of expectations demonstrating that the process of becoming a good supervisor is an ongoing effort.

All of these supervisory skills could not possibly be discussed in the limits of this publication. However, some common concerns of most day care program directors related to specific supervisory processes are addressed, and ideas for the enrichment of employee work experience are offered. Beyond that, day care program directors are encouraged to seek additional readings, training, and personal experiences to perfect their knowledge and capacity to perform in this important area.

The Supervisory Process

Supervision is most easily recognized in some of its specific tasks, such as training and developing staff, evaluating employees, resolving grievances, and correcting unsatisfactory work performance. While we will discuss supervision primarily in terms of these tasks, it is useful to view the subject as a process in which all the components fit together and are governed by common principles. Van Dersal's approach to supervision is built on seven simple but encompassing principles.

1) People must always understand clearly what is expected of them.

2) People must have guidance in doing their work.

3) Good work should always be recognized.

4) Poor work deserves constructive criticism.

5) People should have opportunities to show that they can accept greater responsibilities.

6) People should be encouraged to improve themselves.

7) People should work in a safe and healthful environment.[3]

---

[1] *The Successful Supervisor in Government and Business* (New York: Harper & Row, 1974), p. 10.

[2] *Ibid.*, pp. 8-9.

[3] *Ibid.*, pp. 10-22.

Every employee needs and deserves effective supervision which will provide them feedback about their job performance. For competent employees, it insures that their good performance is recognized. For less-satisfactory employees, it means that mistakes are identified before harm is done to the program and to their self-esteem. Good supervision recognizes that most employees have the potential to improve their skills and that guidance should be provided to help them reach this goal.

Training Staff

The amount of supervision employees receive depends in part on the amount of formal training or experience they have before being hired. In day care, many programs hire workers with limited formal training or experience in child care, so training becomes an important direct responsibility of day care supervisors. Sometimes it is because of financial reasons that the proportion of untrained workers is relatively high; programs might prefer to have staff fully trained in child development or early childhood education but cannot afford them. Sometimes the choice is made out of a belief that workers with a mixture of training, cultural backgrounds, and life experiences should be combined to form a more rounded program for young children.

There are constraints in day care which make it difficult to offer training opportunities to staff. Most day care programs are open more than eight hours each day; they must be kept in operation throughout the year, and licensing regulations require that the caregiving staff be in direct supervision of children at all times. This makes it expensive, complicated, and inconvenient to schedule training opportunities either during the work day or after hours.

Unfortunately, the problems involved in offering staff development programs have led many day care program directors to neglect this subject. However, the need for training is too significant to be given a low priority. In the first place, the care and teaching of children requires considerable knowledge and skill. Second, as Van Dersal's principle states, each employee deserves to know exactly what is expected of her/him. Thus, all the aspects unique to a particular job and the way it is done in a particular day care program need to be taught. Also, there will be new knowledge of the field of child care, improvements in techniques and methods of operating child care programs, and changes in operating policies of employers from time to time. New developments of this nature must be taught to staff. Finally, employees need information which helps them increase their responsibility for existing jobs or prepares them for advancement.

Orientation Training

One component of staff development which is usually the direct responsibility of the day care program director or other top level supervisors is orientation of new employees. Often when a position is vacant, there is a tendency to place the newly employed worker into immediate use. Demands on the other staff when a position is vacant, the cost of substitutes, and staffing requirements of licensing argue for this action. However, at the beginning, when most employees are particularly open to learning, is the right time to teach employees what is expected of them. The anticipation and challenge involved in taking a job has a positive effect on most employees' willingness to consider new information and to accept values or methods which are different from past experience.

Some day care programs have developed formal orientation training programs for new staff which take place before workers are assigned to their duties. More often the orientation training is offered during the first week or two of employment and is interspersed with periods of direct work. The content of the orientation can closely parallel the information recommended in Chapter 3 for inclusion in a program's written policies. Stated briefly, it should cover purpose and history of the day care program and how the program is organized; a description of the personnel policies, salary plan and career development practices of the program; and a thorough discussion of the job including what the duties are, how the job relates to other workers, what authority the job has, and who will supervise the worker. The degree to which orientation training should teach the specific skills or professional practices needed to perform a job will depend on the previous training and experience of a given worker. In those day care positions which do not require much previous training or experience, the orientation should include a heavy concentration on child development theory and techniques and related areas. In some cases, however, new workers prefer an orientation which concentrates on "survival skills"—that is, information which helps them fit into the routine of the organization and perform the specific job with at least a beginning level of efficiency. Thus, it may be useful to postpone those elements of the orientation training which focus on theory or specific program methods until a few weeks after new workers have assumed their duties.

One other major objective of any orientation program is to help new workers feel at ease and begin to gain confidence in themselves and their new organization. This task should receive the personal attention of the worker's immediate supervisor. It should include a tour of the day care program showing work areas, restrooms, where personal belongings can be put, etc., along with introductions to other employees. It should also include periodic visits by supervisors to find out how new employees are performing, and to encourage them to ask questions about things they may not understand.

In-Service Training

In-service training is the education given to employees to improve their work performance. It is the element of staff development which particularly challenges the supervisor's ability to coordinate opportunities and to insure the integration of the content of different training resources. The in-service training program must take into account the various levels of development of individual employees, as well as focus on program-wide objectives. It should be used to strengthen weak program areas, reinforce program strengths, deepen workers' understanding of day care as their experience grows, and introduce new ideas and strategies which allow the program to adapt to changing community needs and professional knowledge.

In recent years the availability of in-service training opportunities for day care programs has increased. Some publicly supported programs have funds especially designated for training, and many such programs are receiving help through contracts with public universities. In other cases, the increased help has come from the wider availability of early childhood training institutions throughout the country and the growing skill of day care program directors to take advantage of the expertise found in the many social, health, and education institutions available in most communities. As this trend continues, the focus of the supervisory role regarding in-service training should be to design an overall plan for training that will insure the conceptual unity of ideas which are presented to staff. Despite these advances, the problem of scheduling training while still keeping programs operating requires that day care supervisors continue to seek innovative techniques of getting information to staff.

Career Development

Career development refers to the concept that programs should prepare employees for positions of increasing responsibility or for long-range career objectives. Career development can be supported both through direct actions of supervisors and general policies of the day care program.

In their daily contact with employees, supervisors should constantly seek to encourage employees' sense of responsibility. For example, when an employee is allowed to perform duties without constant "over-the-shoulder" supervision, feelings of responsibility increase. A second possibility is when an employee is asked to take charge of an aspect of the work of other people (e.g., to help orient a new employee, to teach workers a specific child development technique, etc.). Another alternative is to use opportunities for staff to serve temporarily in more responsible positions. The absence of a director to attend a professional meeting would be a chance to help a lead teacher experience administrative duties for a day or two. Similarly, the illness of a lead teacher could be converted into a positive event by helping a teacher aide assume these duties. Many programs do this already simply because someone has to "fill in" when another staff member is out. However, the real potential of the event is not taken advantage of—employees are not given advance notice enabling them to prepare for the opportunity, and little follow-up discussion is offered to explore whether employees learned from the experience.

In addition, possibilities for advancement should be discussed with employees from time to time in supervisory conferences. Strengths and limitations which affect employees' ability to be promoted to more responsible jobs should be identified. Together the supervisor and employee should plan ways to increase employees' education or job skills so that when promotions are available employees are qualified and fully motivated to fill upgraded positions.

Opportunities for personal growth emerge from the training and information received on the job, but can be promoted by the employer through off-the-job settings also. Programs which can afford it should pay for the cost of courses that staff take. The information staff gains improves job skills and increases their personal mastery in an area of their own interest. Even if the center cannot afford to finance time off or the cost of courses, an effort can be made to schedule work so that staff can get to courses which conflict with hours of program operation. Some programs promote opportunities for employee growth in non-job-related areas. Evening meetings for employees and parents interested in learning a variety of skills (quilting, car repair, family finances, etc.) have been sponsored by day care programs in a number of communities and should be encouraged.

Employee Evaluation

Evaluation of employee performance relates to the principles that employees deserve guidance, praise for accomplishment, and constructive criticism. Evaluation of work performance should be done informally in supervisory conferences throughout the year. In addition, most day care programs require that a more formal evaluation process be conducted once or possibly twice each year. An important policy question which must be decided before a formal evaluation process is instituted is whether the formal evaluation will be used to determine employees' salaries. Some day care programs state that there is a definite relationship between the outcome of formal employee evaluations and salary increases, while others de-emphasize this point recognizing instead the importance of pressure-free evaluation sessions that allow for honest, objective critiques which will contribute to employees' personal and professional growth. Whatever values an individual day care program holds on this topic should be stated clearly for employees and to each individual supervisor responsible for conducting employee evaluation since it is an issue that often causes employee confusion and dissatisfaction.

Most formal employee evaluations are conducted through use of a standard form designed for use with all workers or, more likely, for all workers in a particular job category. Examples of such forms are included in Appendices *F, G* and *H*. Some evaluation forms are designed around requirements contained in the job description, reasoning that these are the tasks, skills and expectations for which employees can justifiably be held accountable. Other forms take on a more introspective character trying to assess personal qualities that contribute to employee effectiveness and career potential.

It is interesting to note how frequently day care program directors express dissatisfaction with the evaluation form they are presently using. They state that they developed a set of evaluation forms, in a few years had to revise them, and are about to revise the forms again—as if to imply their search will be ended when they finally find the ideal employee evaluation form. The likelihood that the forms will be revised periodically should be viewed as positive, rather than the result of an imperfect design of the evaluation instrument. The important element in employee evaluation is the *process* of evaluation, not the tool which serves as the jumping-off place. The assessment should provide an honest and meaningful look at all the strengths and limitations of the worker. From time to time the language on the evaluation form and the scales of measurement (e.g., "Performance is Poor ____ Fair ____ Good ____ Excellent ____.") will become "stale" and will not stimulate the necessary interaction and thoughtful dialogue. It is at just such a time that forms should be revised.

Involving employees in the design of evaluation forms also contributes to the process of insuring their meaningful use. As each job characteristic or quality is discussed and selected for inclusion in the form, employees have an opportunity to look at the broadest possible implications of these attributes for themselves, as well as for their employer. Of equal significance, having a voice in selecting the tool which measures employee performance is democratic and effective motivation for performance at the level of expectation called for by the instrument.

One final note about employee evaluation relates to the concept of probation. "Probation" is a specified period of time (usually from one to six months) during which new workers "try out" the job to see if the type of work and employment conditions are suited to their goals and needs and employers "try out" new workers to determine whether they are suitable under actual working conditions. Probation is mutually useful since it allows either the employer or employees to terminate the employment agreement without hard feelings and, generally, without leaving a mark on employees' records.

This makes the initial evaluation of newly employed workers particularly significant. Generally if an employer chooses to terminate the employment agreement during the probationary period, he or she may do so "without cause," that is, without stating specific reasons why. After the period of probation, it is usually felt that employees have proven that they are satisfactory workers and have earned a right to stay employed unless the employer can cite a specific and reasonable justification for termination.

The period of probation is important for another reason too. Some people are not suited for employment in day care programs—even some people who view it as their chosen field. Characteristics of personality or philosophical expectations of a newly employed worker may simply not match up with the reality of intimate contact with young children on a daily and day-long basis. When this circumstance occurs, day care supervisors have a professional obligation to guide such employees away from day care work. This includes not simply terminating employment but counseling with such workers to see why day care is unsuitable for them, and where appropriate, suggesting fields of employment that would prove productive.

Counseling Employees

Conferences should be scheduled with individual staff members to recognize positive achievements, to identify and support the correction of unsatisfactory behavior, and to arbitrate grievances which employees may have against a specific supervisor or general practices of the employer.

It is desirable that supervisory conferences be regularly scheduled as part of the program's routine. Too often conferences are held only when an employee has done something wrong, and then the whole concept of supervisory conferences loses its potential for promoting positive growth. Praise and recognition for achievement should be a part of the counseling process because it reinforces good behavior. This is a principle which most day care supervisors apply in their work with children but sometimes fail to see that it has equal application with adults. Unlike criticism, which should always be done in private, praise should be given in the presence of other staff when possible.

When the focus of counseling is on some aspect of unsatisfactory work performance, the general approach can either be "supportive" or "disciplinary" and will depend on the severity of the problem, as well as the skills of the supervisor.

The supportive approach applies general knowledge about interpersonal counseling to a work relationship. It seeks to help employees recognize faults or personal problems, prevent discouragement about them, and provide specific help in overcoming the problems. This strategy recognizes that the most acceptable solutions are ones the individual discovers or invents for himself and that supervisors should not try to supply the solution, only the security and encouragement for the search.[4] This is done by a supervisor adopting a "non-judgmental" attitude, that is, by refraining from condemning or being hostile as the worker talks about his behavior; by listening rather than offering direct advice; and by helping the worker clarify the problem in his own mind through encouraging the expression of feelings about the problem as well as discussion of facts.[5]

Counseling of this type can best be done when the supervisor is willing to minimize the degree of authority that exists in the position. Many employers feel they do not have the time or the skill to engage in this form of counseling and that a referral to a professional counseling resource is a more

appropriate action. However, by keeping a supportive approach there are many practical techniques which an employer can use. For example, Dr. Martin R. Feinberg has developed a helpful list of techniques for presenting criticism to employees. They are as follows:

Be involved—Criticize in an environment where you are paying direct attention. Make your problem employee realize that at this moment, he is the most important thing on your mind. Tell him that you have some negative things to say about his performance, but you also have some that are positive.

Say the negative first—The positive should be last because it is part of healing.

Talk about the immediate—If you tell him what it will be like once his troubles are solved, he starts to daydream about how great things are going to be and forgets how he is going to become great.

Take one at a time—If you concentrate on one phase of criticism, he knows what is bothering you.

Never say "always"—This distorts the degree of the person's fault, and helps him to erect a defense against what is really a minor point.

Criticize in the morning, early in the week—By criticizing at the beginning of the week, early in the day, you give yourself a chance to relate, to build a strong, constructive, improving relationship.

Steer clear of humor—It will be interpreted as sarcasm.

Be specific—In your criticism.

Heal with praise—Try to close the interview with a word on a positive subject; do not exaggerate, because it will reflect on judgment.[6]

Disciplinary counseling of employees has as its purpose to foster a feeling of mutual respect between supervisor and staff, to keep employees satisfied while at the same time getting them to conduct themselves in accordance with established rules of the employer, and to train staff to perform their duties efficiently, being sure that supervisory instructions are clear and understood.[7]

It is important to recognize that disciplinary counseling is designed to promote *corrective action,* not punishment. Penalties should be used

---

[4]Dr. Mark B. Silber, *Managing the Problem Employee* (available from Hume-Silber Associates, Ltd., 228 North La Salle Street, Chicago, Illinois 60601), p. 8.

[5]*Ibid.,* p. 7.

[6]*Business Management,* July 1964, p. 36.

[7]Earl R. Bramblett, "Maintenance of Discipline," *Management of Personnel Quarterly,* Volume 1, Number 1, Autumn, 1961, p. 10.

only when an offense is serious and when the motivation of revenge or vindictiveness is absent.[8] Supervisors who apply disciplinary measures for violation of rules should insure that rules and instructions are simple and understandable. They should know the rules themselves and should act promptly when a violation occurs. All relevant facts should be gathered and employees should have the opportunity to explain their position. If it is decided that disciplinary action is needed (e.g., suspension without pay, return to probationary status, demotion), it should be done in accordance with established program policy; including the opportunity to appeal the decision when appropriate. Finally, any disciplinary action should be accurately documented and signed by the supervisor and employee involved.

Dismissing an Employee

Sooner or later every supervisor encounters that fateful moment when a decision must be made whether to retain or discharge a worker. In studies among large industries, Steinmetz learned that very few workers are ever fired. They are either promoted, demoted, transferred, retired or dehired.[9] "Dehiring" refers to the practice of making work life so unsatisfactory for the employee that he/she chooses to resign. While this practice may seem unethical, Steinmetz argues that under certain circumstances it can be humane and offers the opportunity for workers to maintain their self-esteem.[10]

The reluctance to fire employees, even among supposedly impersonal large corporations, may be explained by the many factors that must be weighed in making this decision. Steinmetz describes 11 issues which could have important bearing on whether to discharge or retain a worker. They are: 1) employee's length of service with the organization; 2) employee performance record—

the potential to save an employee is good if they have an overall good performance record and their work has only recently fallen off; 3) skills involved and the labor market demand for the skill; 4) absenteeism record; 5) employee attitude and personality; 6) employee's level of responsibility in the organization; 7) adequacy of the supervision received by the employee; 8) legal job security mechanisms—alternative methods available for the employee to appeal dismissal and whether the employee would use them or not; 9) investment in the employee—money, time and training; 10) personal consequences to the employee; and 11) effect of the firing on other employees—could be negative because it lowers morale of workers who feel threatened by the action or could be positive if it removes a worker whose actions are resented by other employees.[11]

The decision to fire an employee may be precipitated by a single "last straw" event, but it should not be made in anger and it usually should be made when several of these 11 factors combine to forge an overwhelming argument for dismissal. When employers first suspect that a serious disciplinary action or even dismissal may be required, they should begin to document the problem and steps that have been taken to correct the employee's unsatisfactory performance. Most employer-operated structures for resolving employee grievances as well as the judicial process expect that the employer will cite specific incidents and reasons for firing the worker and that the employer will demonstrate that commonly accepted supervisory practices (e.g., conferences with employee, written warnings, etc.) were used prior to the dismissal action. It is not necessary for an employer to record in the personnel file every unsatisfactory action of every employee, but it is necessary to document a clear pattern of problems and employer intervention in cases of those employees where dismissal may be one possible alternative.

[8]Lawrence L. Steinmetz, *Managing the Marginal and Unsatisfactory Performer* (Reading, Massachusetts: Addison Wesley Publishing Company, 1969), p. 85.

[9]*Ibid.,* p. 47.

[10]*Ibid.,* p. 130.

[11]*Ibid.,* pp. 48-50.

CHAPTER 8
Employee Motivation

What motivates people to work to their full capacity? What can an employer do to create an environment in which highly motivated employees will develop and thrive? Textbooks about personnel management usually discuss concepts of employee motivation in a chapter devoted to supervision and supervisory techniques. In this publication, the subject of employee motivation has been reserved for a concluding chapter. The investigation of issues in employee motivation extends well beyond the role of the immediate supervisor and helps to draw together some of the important concerns and ideas expressed throughout this publication.

Frederick Hertzberg is one of the best known researchers in the field of employee motivation. His studies of factors which create job dissatisfaction and job satisfaction have led to several important conclusions. Factors which lead to job dissatisfaction are mostly centered in the work environment. The most common dissatisfying factors include: company policy and administration, supervision, interpersonal relationships, working conditions, salary, status, and security. While some reasonable effort should be made to improve all these areas of work life, Hertzberg points out that removal of these barriers does not necessarily result in job satisfaction. Instead there is a different set of factors which contribute to job satisfaction and which affects employee motivation. The job-satisfying factors are much more related to the actual content of the job. They include: the work itself, responsibility, achievement, recognition for achievement, and growth or advancement.[1] Hertzberg's work was done in industrial and business settings but much of this information applies to day care and other human service endeavors.

Dissatisfying Factors

It is difficult for a day care program director or other immediate supervisor to change any of the dissatisfying factors.

Company Policy and Administration

All organizations have rules and procedures which govern the conduct of work and the employer/employee relationship. This publication has stressed the importance of putting those rules in writing so that this significant area of information is readily available and easily understood. Beyond this action, day care employers should give thought to involving employees in decision-making. This is a suggestion which recognizes that day care organizations should avoid the extremes of either being highly authoritarian or being so democratic as to be leaderless. Instead, what is suggested is that participation in decisions is a healthy process for employees and organizations, and that most day care programs should give greater attention to ways in which employee ideas can be used in the process of planning and those areas of program management which lend themselves to employee critique and suggestion. In a similar vein, there is a need to be self-critical about the quality of overall leadership in day care programs. If there is competition among leaders, if there is duplication of effort, or if there are other forms of waste and inefficiency, it will become apparent to employees at every level of the program. Often the resulting job dissatisfaction is not perceived to be the product of weakness in company policy and administration but is attributed to a variety of other causes. Fortunately, there

---

[1] "One More Time, How Do You Motivate Employees," *Harvard Business Review*, January-February, 1968, pp. 35-44. See also the discussion of Hertzberg's ideas in *The Successful Supervisor in Government and Business*, 3rd ed., by William Van Dersal, Harper & Row, New York, 1974.

is a trend among day care program directors to seek out training and information about administrative theory and methods. This positive development should be encouraged at institutions which train day care professionals and through continuing education activities sponsored by day care professional organizations.

Supervision

Hertzberg points out that there are two distinct components of supervision, each of which could lead to job dissatisfaction. The *technical* component of supervision refers to the job competency of supervisors. That is, the supervisors' knowledge of the job to be done, the stress they place on training, their ability to teach employees, and their general method of seeing that the responsibilities of the unit are carried out. Recognizing that inadequate technical supervision leads to job dissatisfaction reinforces what has already been said about the importance of training for day care workers. In addition, at the individual supervisory level, it calls for supervisors who give sufficient instruction for each task, who are able to delegate responsibility, who delineate each employee's duties, who keep staff informed of developments in the organization and who are open to new ideas and changes in program.

The *interpersonal* component of supervision refers to the social relationship between supervisor and workers. Supervisors who are abrupt, moody, sarcastic, egotistical, or lack interest in their employees will contribute to job dissatisfaction. Similarly a supervisor who breaks rules others must follow, who allows anger at one employee to affect his judgment of others, or who takes advantage of good workers, will end up with dissatisfied employees. Recognizing one's personal imperfection is difficult and is usually accomplished through the aid of a second person, either a friend or, in most larger organizations, an objective but empathetic supervisor higher up in the chain of command. Day care programs are sometimes unable to supply the help a supervisor needs to grow in this area. In some communities, day care "support groups" have developed. These are voluntary groups of directors and/or center employees representing several day care programs. While such groups have several objectives, the nurturance of a supervisor's personal development is an important goal. Creation of support groups in other communities should be encouraged.

Interpersonal Relations

Poor social relations among fellow workers or poor family and other non-work related personal relationships can affect job satisfaction. The role of the employer in helping a worker with such problems presents some difficult questions. Aspects of personality, such as whether an employee is moody, shy, lazy, or short-tempered, affect job satisfaction and can affect productivity of the entire work group. Similarly, more serious personal problems—a deterioration in physical health, abuse of alcohol or drugs, marital break up, etc.,—can become a source of subsequent poor job performance.

Most day care directors show an admirable degree of concern for employees' personal problems and employees can usually count on being given the benefit of the doubt. At the same time, some workers are beginning to argue that a line needs to be drawn somewhere so that the right to privacy is maintained. This is an issue which will require further study although, overall, the appropriate action seems to call for an increase in day care program directors' ability to understand adult problems of living coupled with more frequent referral of employees to outside counseling resources.

Working Conditions

This characteristic has to do with the need for a safe and healthy work environment, whether the worksite is conveniently located or not, and the amount of work expected. In day care, the degree of regulation of physical conditions (sanitation, fire safety, etc.) is quite extensive so there are not likely to be many unsafe factors. However, most of the space in the facility is taken up with child care materials and there is sometimes a failure to provide space for employees' needs. Places to put purses or other personal articles, an area to take a break and get completely away from the children are the kinds of physical conditions which should be taken into consideration by more day care programs.

Salary

Salary would seem to belong in the job satisfaction category but, in fact, this factor can be an influence in either direction. However, even as a source of satisfaction, employees often describe salary not as an end in itself but as an item which contributes to a sense of achievement, recognition and advancement. As a job-dissatisfying factor, salary is mentioned in relation to the way in which the system of salaries is administered. A system which gives increases reluctantly, does not differentiate between new and experienced employees, and is not built on some objective basis will sooner or later prove unacceptable.

Status

The care of children is a relatively low status profession. Most directors know of staff who have left this field for work in another profession of presumably higher status. They also know of employees who have tried unsuccessfully to find employment in some other field and who have accepted a day care position only out of economic necessity. A day care employer must be able to acknowledge the facts of the situation with staff as a whole and pay attention to individual employees whose dissatisfaction is high. For some, the advice should be to change jobs, while for others it is possible to demonstrate the many satisfying characteristics of day care employment. At the same time, day care program directors must devote part of their time in leadership activities which promote day care as a profession. Until recently, participation in community activities and public relations work in support of day care have not been viewed as important by many directors. However, these are important activities which demonstrate to staff that their employer supports their efforts to achieve professional status.

Security

The relationship of benefit programs and employee feelings of security is described in detail in Chapter 5. Another dimension of security relates to knowing that a given job will continue to be needed and that the day care program will continue to operate and supply employment. This kind of anxiety arises from strained economic conditions and from changes of policy of federal and state agencies which provide public funds to purchase day care. While a day care program director may feel that these are circumstances beyond his or her control, he or she must be prepared to deal with the consequences in relation to employees. The financial condition and organizational health of a day care program is usually a subject discussed only by the owner or board of directors who have responsibility for these issues. However, it should be recognized that a center which abolishes positions due to changes in public policy or eliminates staff to cut expenses will have a demoralized workforce. To minimize the staff dissatisfaction over this issue, program leaders will need to pursue a relatively frank and honest policy related to financial and organizational well-being. Admittedly this approach has problems. Sometimes, in the early phases of budget planning, a situation looks bad and then improves as the facts become more clear. It is difficult to decide how soon and in what detail discussions of the financial condition of the program should be held. While there can be no sure guidelines, each program must recognize the need to communicate with staff on this topic and the consequences in employee dissatisfaction that surround the problem.

Job Satisfaction

The day care program director has greater control over factors which contribute to job satisfaction so that this is an area in which he or she can be particularly helpful. At the same time, it is usually an area in which less thought is given and, consequently, few day care programs have devoted the time and imagination to realize the full potential of efforts to increase job satisfaction.

The Work Itself

Fortunately, for most people who enter day care, the very nature of the work is appealing. They enjoy the daily emotional, physical, and intellectual interactions which take place between themselves and the children in their care, and they appreciate the opportunity to work with parents in supporting a stable, healthy, family environment. However, a day care program director can do much to enhance this satisfaction.

First, aspects of day care work which are boring, repetitious, or unpleasant should be recognized and efforts made to lessen their impact. This could occur in a variety of ways and will vary with the characteristics of each program. Attention should be paid to the availability of breaks, the scheduling of shifts, and changes in classroom assignments. Rotating or shifting of unpleasant duties is another possibility, although it should be recognized that simple redistribution of an unpleasant duty will not convert the duty into a positive activity.

Second, the day care program director should help staff recognize that their job is part of a "larger picture." Most directors recognize that staff should understand how their individual jobs contribute to the overall operation of the program, but few directors give attention to communicating with staff about the day care program's contribution to the well-being of families and the nation as a whole. Such an effort can be made without sounding grandiose or falsely optimistic. It can include sharing information with staff about policy and legislative issues that are happening at the federal, state, or local level, making literature available about the need for or impact of day care, and encouraging staff to participate in professional activities.

The third area which directors should consider is "job enrichment."[2] This concept attempts to increase employees' personal contribution to their existing job. While some activities in this direction are simple and immediately fruitful, others call for a reconceptualization of how each job should be performed or how the program should operate. At its simplest level, job enrichment can be done by introducing new and more difficult tasks not previously handled or enabling a staff member to become an expert in a given topic. For example, an aide can be asked to take responsibility for planning the daily program for a week, or a teacher could be assigned to study the subject of outdoor play and make recommendations on equipment and the outdoor routine. At a complex level, day care programs may wish to intensify study of early childhood program design. The many alternative approaches to curriculum which were researched and developed in the late 1960s have not been extensively adopted in day care as yet. There is a great deal of potential for directors and staff to consider new theoretical approaches which could lead to changes in job roles and provide additional skills to day care workers.

Responsibility

Responsibility is clearly allied with job enrichment since it can involve added duties and greater participation in the day care program's operation. As supervisors decide how closely to supervise workers and as they use imagination in selecting assignments they can bring about an increase in workers' responsibilities. Most day care program directors recognize that growth in responsibility is an objective of their work with some lower level supervisors (e.g., lead teachers and cooks who oversee the work of assistant cooks). However, it would be helpful for supervisors to apply this attitude toward all staff. The capability and potential of people who join an organization at entry level positions are often overlooked, and many day care programs would benefit by a conscious effort to support a growth in responsibility among these workers.

Achievement

A sense of achievement was the item mentioned most often in the Hertzberg studies of job satisfaction factors. Undoubtedly, a sense of achievement comes from having responsibility for an interesting job and specific instances of feeling accomplishment for work well done.

In day care, staff may not always realize their achievements. Growth in children can take place so subtly that it may not be recognized. Program strengths or improvements in operation may not seem significant to staff who are isolated in a program where there is no basis for comparison. One step many day care programs have taken is to develop a system for evaluating children's progress. This practice is highly recommended since it improves planning for the children's needs and helps employees recognize growth and changes in children as a result of their work. Fewer day care programs have developed approaches to evaluation of the overall program and, in fact, there are few professional resources for effective program-wide evaluation. Of those programs that do use a process of program evaluation, the design is often geared to the accountability needs of funding bodies or to the policy interests of social scientists, and thus does not speak in the practical terms helpful to employees. Day care programs need to take some initiative in this area so that more examples of appropriate program wide evaluation techniques are available.

Recognition For For Achievement

While systems for evaluation help staff recognize their own achievements, recognition by others is a powerful reinforcer of that accomplishment. Whatever people achieve, either a specific action or a long continued and sustained effort, recognition ought to be prompt and clear. Much of the responsibility for making sure that recognition is given rests in the hands of the day care director and other supervisors.

Chances for recognition from other people significant to the day care program are important also. Parents should be encouraged to share with staff observations about how their children have grown as a result of the program. Board members or other community people who are familiar with the program's work could be invited to speak at a special event in honor of the staff; certificates or some form of reward could be given to those employees who have provided special services.

Growth or Advancement

It is interesting to note that the good feeling people expressed from experiencing one of the five satisfying factors lasts a long time after the specific events involved. This was especially true concerning the factors of work itself, responsibility, and advancement.[3] Advancement may not be easy to

[2] *Ibid.*, p. 41.

[3] Van Dersal, p. 64.

obtain in day care. In a small program there may be only a few upper-level positions and vacancies may not occur often. These limitations should be acknowledged to staff, however, the director should use the suggestions made on supervision to prepare staff for advancement.

It should also be emphasized that sometimes advancement occurs only when an employee leaves for a more responsible job in another day care program. Some directors are not willing to accept this idea since it involves losing an employee who is an effective contributor and in whom considerable training and concern have been invested. But, the other side of the issue is that employees may regress if they are not able to advance when they are ready. They become bored, unchallenged, and lose enthusiasm. This is one of the circumstances which leads to the condition of worker "burn out" which is a growing problem in many human service fields.[4]

Helping an employee advance by facilitating and encouraging employment at another program raises another question. Some day care programs view themselves as being in direct competition with other day care programs—competition for children, competition for financial resources, and competition for qualified staff. Currently there are economic and political realities which threaten the survival of day care programs. Under these circumstances it is perhaps an understandable reaction to compete and attempt to win. Yet it must also be pointed out that the solution does not lie in the doctrine of "survival of the fittest." Part of the resolution must come through actions of mutual cooperation and support. Many day care programs feel relatively isolated from other day care programs even in their own community. Mechanisms need to be developed to encourage discussion and understanding among all types of day care programs. This is a necessary preliminary step before day care professionals can successfully advocate for better public policy toward families and toward day care in general. This mutual cooperation should take place in day-to-day activities. It includes sharing of information so that the special needs of a child or parent can best be served. And it means insuring that employees who have grown immensely under the guidance and encouragement of one day care program will have a chance to become day care leaders, no matter where the opportunity and need for leadership exists.

---

[4]For a complete discussion of this topic see: Stanley Siederman, "Combating Staff Burn-Out," *Day Care and Early Education,* Summer, 1978.

APPENDIX A
Statement of Goals and Objectives
(Sample)

Background: This statement was developed in 1970 at the beginning of a project that involved eight states and included the provision of day care to various age groups (infants through school-age children), through different forms (center care and family day care), and through different operating agencies (state agency, not-for-profit, for-profit). Therefore, it is not to be considered as an example of the goals and objectives for a single program.

Goals

I. Day care is concerned with the child's total growth and development. It should promote his/her physical development, help him/her to become socially competent in relating to adults as well as to peers, encourage emotional growth and control, and provide opportunity for the cognitive learnings which are so crucial during the early years. All of these aspects of the child's development need to be carefully planned for and periodically assessed.

II. Day care is concerned with the development of children's skills. This includes social skills (consideration for others, cooperation); psychological skills (expressiveness, self-sufficiency, maleness or femaleness); physical skills (running, climbing); and learning skills (ideas, words, colors, numbers, problem-solving).

III. Day care is a basic support to the family. It aims to enhance and expand the parents' relationship with the child. This philosophy is understood and shared with all members of the staff. Training should sensitize staff to the dangers of unconsciously undermining the parental role, and it should provide staff with positive techniques for enhancing it. Day care does not substitute, compete with, or disparage the role of parents.

IV. Day care strives to make families more effective by assisting and encouraging them to correct any significant physical problems in the children, to provide a balanced diet, and to take advantage of appropriate health services. Parents are helped to recognize and reinforce behaviors which lead to the acquisition of social, physical, and cognitive skills while the child is at home. Day care as a basic support to families should involve parents in making decisions about hours of operation, intake policy, educational objectives, health and social services, fees charged, staffing, and the like, to as great a degree as possible.

V. Day care programs should be community-based. They should utilize the strength and resources of the neighborhood and be aware of and responsive to the community's needs and problems.

VI. Day care should make every effort to serve families with different economic, cultural, and ethnic backgrounds and to prevent segregation on the basis of any of these factors.

VII. Day care staff members should be drawn from various ethnic and cultural backgrounds. Staff should include professionals, paraprofessionals, and community people, including parents of children in the program. There should be a program of staff development with opportunities for career advancement.

Objectives for Children

I. To promote the healthy growth and development of each preschool child according to his/her own potential in the following areas:

A. *Physical development*—to promote each child's growth and general health.
   1. The recommended immunization program is completed for each child.
   2. Abnormal physical conditions are detected.
   3. Each child makes progress toward ideal height and weight norms.
B. *Social and emotional development*—to help each child gain social and personal adjustment needed for daily living.
   1. Child develops self-esteem as manifested by positive sense of self-identification.
   2. Child demonstrates self-confidence in relationships with adults by asking for help when needed and seeking affection when desired.
   3. Child demonstrates self-confidence in relationships with other children by planning, sharing and, when necessary, protecting him/herself.
   4. Child develops ability to understand and manage his/her emotions—frustration, fear, rage, joy, etc.
   5. Child develops an increasing sense of responsibility appropriate for his/her age.
   6. Child develops persistence in completing a task and in the ability to concentrate for increasing periods of time.
   7. Child develops a sense of time as to when activities and events occur and recur in the daily schedule.
   8. Objectionable behavior patterns which affect the child's acceptance of him/herself and by others are identified and modified.
C. *Motor skills*—to help each child develop body and manual coordination appropriate for his/her age.
   1. Child develops progressively complicated gross motor skills, such as walking, stair-climbing, running, hopping, dancing, and playing ball.
   2. Child develops progressively complicated manual coordination from initial ability to grasp to eventual use of simple tools, such as crayons, scissors, hammer, etc.
D. *Intellectual development*—to aid each child to develop language skills, problem-solving ability and perception.
   1. Child develops verbal and communication skills as evidenced by use of growing vocabulary, connected sentences, plurals, and understandable speech.
   2. Child develops number concepts as manifested by knowing his/her age, its magnitude relative to other children's ages, counting of objects and relationships of "more" or "less."
   3. Child develops understanding of abstract concepts such as "over and under," "up and down," "sooner and later," "near and far," etc.
   4. Child develops color discrimination as manifested by ability to sort and match objects by color and to name various colors.
E. *Development of creativity*—to aid each child to develop creative potential.
   1. Child uses materials provided by center (such as paper, paints, wood, blocks, etc.) to create designs and objects.
   2. Child displays imagination, as in dramatic play, storytelling, etc.
F. *Development of self-help skills*—to help each child develop skill and independence in caring for him/herself.
   1. Child learns to feed him/herself and to use eating and drinking utensils properly.
   2. Child learns to dress him/herself, to wash, use toothbrush and to assume responsibility for toileting, according to age.
II. To provide care for the school-age child (when school is not in session and parents are absent from home) that will supplement and enrich the activities of home, neighborhood, and school.
   A. *Child is provided with care and protection after school and at other times when parents are working and school is not in session.*
   B. *Each child is helped to gain the social and personal adjustment needed for daily living.*
      1. Child assumes sense of responsibility as evidenced by arriving at day care facility on time, if distance permits, and by executing short errands or trips into the community as appropriate for his/her age.
      2. Child learns to make a purposeful choice of available after-school activities and initiates such activities without undue prodding.
      3. Child forms relationships with one or more children in the group.
      4. Child is helpful and supportive to other children, especially younger children, in the day care center.

C. *To provide support for the formal cognitive development of school-age children.*
  1. Child obtains support in homework or other intellectual interests through availability of quiet times, reference materials, trips to the library, books, and tutorial help or other assistance if needed and desired.
  2. Child participates in a variety of community experiences that broaden perspectives and horizons (field trips, cultural and other entertainment, or learning events).
D. *To help each child to develop skills in appropriate sports or games.*
  1. Child learns the rudiments or skills of a sport or game appropriate for age or sex.
E. *To aid each child to develop creative potential.*
  1. Child produces small gifts or other objects using materials available at the day care facility.
  2. Child is given opportunity to pursue a talent or interest in art, music, drama or writing, and accomplishments are recognized, appreciated and supported.

Objectives for Families

I. To meet the needs of the family for day care services.
  A. *The day care center either directly meets the child care needs of the family by enrolling the children who require care, or by making suitable arrangements for care of children who are not accommodated directly by the center.*
II. To strengthen parents in their relationships with their children.
  A. *By encouraging them to assume responsibility for their own children in relation to day care.*
    1. Parents make an effort to bring the child to or pick him/her up from the day care center at a time predetermined jointly and as feasible in each individual case.
    2. Parents follow through on appointments with doctors and dentists or other medical services that might have been determined to be the parent's responsibility in completing the child's health program.
    3. Parents follow through on confer-

ences arranged by day care center to discuss child and day care program; the center plans the conferences to be held at times convenient for parents.
    4. Parents follow through on agreed-upon volunteer assignments when given opportunity (provided parent is not working and has time). Volunteer assignments should cover a wide range of activities from sending cookies to the day care center to spending time in the center to assist teachers.
  B. *By helping families to improve their living patterns at home to provide for the healthy development of their children.*
    1. Parents talk with and listen to child about his/her experiences and interests.
    2. Family uses more positive and consistent methods of discipline.
    3. Family shows evidence of cherishing children's accomplishments (pictures children have produced or other handiwork they bring home).
    4. Family encourages use of educational materials in the home (crayons, library books if available, storybooks or catalogs to look at pictures).
    5. Family sets aside homework time for older children and provides best possible conditions for study (quiet, place, privacy).
    6. Family observes regular bedtimes for children.
    7. Meal patterns in home are regular (regular meals including a variety of foods instead of snacks).
    8. Family removes obvious hazards that may exist in the home.
    9. Family treats children with respect and fosters an attitude of self-worth in children.
III. To strengthen parents' role as members of their communities and as partners in the day care program.
  A. *By providing parents an opportunity to participate in the planning and implementation of the day care program for their children.*
    1. Parents make up at least half of the Advisory Committee members.
    2. Parents are elected by other parents to represent them on community committees, state committees, and other groups concerned with programs for young children.
    3. Parents participate in making policy on admissions, fees, hours of oper-

ation, and programs to be offered by day care for children and parents.

B. *By encouraging parents to avail themselves of a variety of opportunities to have contact with day care programs at times and locations convenient to parents.*
  1. Parents participate in conferences that are arranged to suit both parents and day care staff.
  2. The kinds of opportunities for parents to do volunteer work in the center are based on the parents' availability, skills and needs.
  3. Center provides periodic communication with families and promotes mutual confidence between the center and the parents. (Examples might be the exchange of recipes or a newsletter from the center to the families.)

Objectives for Communities

I. To promote community understanding of quality day care services.
  1. Community leadership (including unions and employers) gains an understanding through advisory committees of the problems of working mothers and the community's needs in day care services.
  2. Volunteers from various community

groups aid in the center's day care program.
  3. Evidence of public concern about the day care project and general day care needs is manifested through newspaper articles, letters to editors, inquiries from community, and other public news media.
  4. Community members donate money, equipment, or service to the day care center.

II. To provide families and children a resource which could reduce child abuse or neglect and juvenile offenses, and which could provide an alternative to removing children from their own homes when such problems exist.
  1. Children who might otherwise have been placed in foster homes are enrolled in day care programs.
  2. Agency records and personnel indicate the reporting of suspected abuse or neglect when appropriate.

III. To initiate and implement communication and cooperation between day care and other educational programs, such as kindergarten, ESEA schools and first grades.
  1. Day care staff visits neighborhood schools for follow-up of day care children or for other purposes.
  2. Joint use of facilities, training, and workshops, where applicable, by various programs.
  3. School personnel visit day care programs.
  4. Mothers and children are introduced to school with day care staff assistance, if needed.

APPENDIX B

Outline for
a Parent Policy Handbook

I. Goals and Organization of the Day Care Program.
A parent handbook should include the goals of the program and the administration's attitude toward early childhood development. This section should also describe the program—how it is governed, funded, and licensed, what is the address and telephone number, and how parents can be involved.

II. Policies of Operation.
A second section should cover the daily policies of the program. The following topics might be considered.

A. *Hours and Admission Policies*
This includes the daily opening and closing times, when the program is closed for holidays or vacation, policies on whether the child will remain enrolled during periods of prolonged absence (due to illness or parent vacation), policy on when a child arrives late in the morning, policy on when parents are late picking up a child, and a statement requesting that the program be notified when a child will be absent because of a family emergency.

B. *Custody of a Child*
This includes process for verifying legal custody of a child (if appropriate), request that parents bring child into the building and not just leave child at the door, requirement that parents notify center in advance if anyone other than parent comes for child, and request for telephone and address of parents so that they can be contacted if a problem arises.

C. *Daily Program and Routines*
1. Description of the daily schedule including kinds of activities child will

experience and where to find a posted schedule of activities.

2. Description of the type of field trips offered, written permission required, and when and how trips will be announced.

3. Explanation of meal program including which meals are offered (breakfast, morning snack, lunch, etc.), how meals are served (family style, cafeteria style) and why, how children with special diets are served, and whether or not parents with infants must supply food or formula.

4. Explanation of nap time procedures.

5. Policies for handling child discipline including an explanation of how setting limits can help a child, what discipline practices are not used and why (e.g., spanking, denial of food), and what practices are used and why (e.g., praise, short separation from group).

6. Discussion of policies on potty training.

D. *Health Procedures*
1. This area includes requirements for health history prior to enrollment, policy on daily health inspection upon arrival, policy on whether a sick child will be accepted or must stay at home, policy on whether the center will administer prescription and/or over-the-counter medicines, signed permission to obtain emergency medical attention, telephone where parent(s) can be reached, where doctor can be reached, and the names of additional

people to be contacted in case of a medical emergency.

2) An explanation of medical and liability insurance carried by and/or available through the day care program.

E. *Child Personal Items*

This includes discussion of the type of clothes to wear, whether a change of clothes is required, whether program or parents will supply diapers, whether clothes must be labeled, and condition under which toys, candy, or money are permitted.

F. *Parent/Day Care Program Responsibilities*

1. A discussion of how parent conferences are scheduled both for regular and special purposes, a discussion of how parent volunteer work can be used, and a discussion of how parent complaints will be handled.

2. Description of how fee is determined, and when fee is due.

3. Description of records kept by the program related to the child (attendance, health, individual development).

4. A description of the state law related to child abuse and the responsibility of the day care program to report child abuse.

APPENDIX C

Outline of Topics to be Included in an Operations Manual

I. Information About the Conduct of Major Tasks of Program Operation
   A. *Admission Policies*—Fee policies and criteria for enrolling a child, procedures for completing the enrollment process, procedures for maintaining a waiting list.
   B. *Education Philosophy and Daily Plan*—Discussion of the specific educational philosophy of the program (e.g., Open Education, Montessori, etc.) and how those beliefs are to be implemented through a planned program of daily activities.
   C. *Grouping*—Plan for grouping children (i.e., all 3 year-olds together vs. a mixed age group), under what circumstances a child should change a group, maximum size of each group.
   D. *Materials*—Description of how child development materials and equipment are to be used and cared for.
   E. *Building*—Description of how to schedule use of space (e.g., when various age groups will be on the playground or whether all children will eat lunch at the same time or not), policies on maintaining the cleanliness of the facility, and who is responsible for various maintenance chores.
   F. *Special Child Arrangements*—How to handle mealtime, nap, outdoor play, bathroom periods, field trips, etc.
   G. *Health and Safety*—Procedures for daily health inspections, staff assignments, and instruction during emergencies (injury to a child, fire, severe weather, etc.), first aid information, accident-preventing restrictions on child behavior or use of facility, procedures designed to prevent spread of disease, and policy on accepting or caring for a sick child.

   H. *Parents and Community*—Policies of communication and cooperation with parents, discussion of practices to maintain good public relations, specific staff assignments to work with volunteers, staff assignments to coordinate with other day care programs or other community agencies.
   I. *Record Keeping*—Procedures for evaluating individual children, maintaining child records, policies on referring children to social and health service agencies.
   J. *Business Practices*—Designation of staff authorized to purchase materials or receive money, procedures for inventory or storage of materials, procedure for maintaining licensing status.
   K. *Transportation*—For centers with a vehicle, there should be detailed instructions about the operation and maintenance of the vehicle, a set of safety practices, procedures to be followed if an accident occurs, first aid instructions, and information about safety equipment to be maintained on the vehicle (first aid kit, fire extinguisher).

II. Instructions to Staff on Appropriate Attitudes and Behavior to Promote the Development of Children
   Most programs provide staff with instructions related to the growth and development of children. This usually includes information on "ages and stages," policies on child discipline, and discussion of attitudes to be displayed by adults and encouraged in children.

III. *Instructions to Staff Concerning the Conduct of Their Specific Job*
   This information varies depending on how roles are divided. For example, a day care program where the owner or director also keeps the books will record less about this

function than one with a separate book-keeper. In general, each job has many more tasks than can be squeezed into a job description. Information about completion of various forms or the details of a fairly complex process should be included here.

For cooks, this could include procedures on purchase, storage and preparation of food.

For accountants or bookkeepers, it would include procedures related to purchasing, payroll preparation, property inventory, financial reporting, etc. For transportation workers, it usually includes specific instructions on safety practices and vehicle maintenance.

APPENDIX D

Outline of Topics to be Included in the Personnel Policies and Procedures of a Day Care Program

I. Statement of Employer Philosophy Toward Employees

II. Process for Establishment and Amendment of Personnel Policies
   A. Description of how a board of directors or its personnel committee will work with staff in the development of personnel policies.
   B. Statement of how often the policies will be reviewed.

III. Employment and Employee Status
   A. A definition of the types of employee status. Permanent and probationary employees are the most common. It may be desirable to define or discuss temporary employee status (e.g., a substitute teacher) and the terms promotion and transfer.
   B. A statement that the program is an equal opportunity employer.
   C. A description of the process by which a vacancy is filled.
   D. A description of the process for resigning, and the required period of notice.
   E. The policy regarding retirement.

IV. Basic Employment Description and Expectation
   This includes the length of the workday and workweek; policy for documenting time; statement about when salaries are paid; recommendations or requirements concerning type of clothes to wear; areas in the building in which smoking is permitted or prohibited; whether staff are expected to eat lunch with the children (required in the day care licensing standards in some states) or are permitted a separate lunch period; if desirable, a statement prohibiting employees from eating or drinking foods which the children do not have (e.g., eating candy or coke in the classroom); a statement of health tests (TB, physical, VD, etc.) which may be required for employment in day care; information about parking, or areas of the building which can be used for breaks or planning work; and policies on use of the telephone for personal calls.

V. Salary Plan and Description of Fringe Benefits
   A. Included in the salary plan should be a statement of the employer's philosophy on salaries, how base salaries are established and are reviewed, and under what conditions salary increases will be made available.
   B. Included in the fringe benefit discussion should be a description of required fringe benefits (usually workman's compensation, unemployment insurance and social security) and a description of optional fringe benefits (e.g., medical insurance, life insurance, retirement plan). Information about the pros and cons of choosing various optional fringe benefits should be available and could be included in the Personnel Policies and Procedures document.

VI. Attendance and Leave
   A. Definition of expectations regarding regular attendance, procedure for notifying if employee will be late, policy when an employee is absent without authorization.
   B. Definition of vacation and sick leave—how it is accumulated, whether unused leave may be carried over at the end of a year, how soon to apply in advance for

vacation leave, whether sick leave must be documented by a doctor's statement, definition of other family members whose illness would justify the use of sick leave.
C. Definition of leave for special purposes, such as jury duty, voting, serving as an election officer, and attending a funeral. Some programs have a policy to cover when the program is closed due to bad weather.
D. Definition of educational leave where applicable.
E. Definition of maternity leave.

VII. Disciplinary Actions and Appeal Procedure
A. This should include a description of the process by which discipline will be administered. It could include the steps of probation, suspension, and dismissal, although often it only includes a dismissal process.
B. The actions of an employee which could cause a dismissal should be stated. Some of the most common reasons are: The employee uses physical force in disciplining child, the employee has falsified employment information, consistent failure to carry out assigned duties, failure to comply with the program's licensure regulations and, in some programs, the violation of confidential information— such as discussing a child's behavior with someone other than staff or a child's parents.
C. A description of how an individual employee may appeal a disciplinary action or other decision related to employment.

D. A description of how general grievances of employees can be brought to the attention of an upper level of supervision or the board.

VIII. Employee Evaluation
A process of periodic evaluation of employee performance is common in most day care programs. Discussion should include purposes of the evaluation, its frequency, whether the evaluation will or will not be used in making decisions about promotion or salary increases, and usually a statement that the employee is required to sign the evaluation.

IX. Miscellaneous Topics
Other possible subjects that some day care programs have found necessary to include are:
A. Policies related to nepotism—that is, whether relatives of current employees or board members can be hired or be the supervisor of a relative.
B. Policies of what kinds of political activities an employee can engage in; this only applies to centers which are subject to certain federal laws (Chapter 15, Title V of the United States Code—formerly known as the Hatch Act—and/or Sections 606 (6) and 213 of the Economic Opportunity Act).
C. Special meetings or workshops which employees are expected to attend.
D. Policies of whether an employee's child can be enrolled in the program or not.
E. Statement related to employees' travel and conditions under which they will be reimbursed for expenses.

APPENDIX E
Sample Job Descriptions

The sample job descriptions which follow are reproduced with permission of Day Care Services, Inc., of Birmingham, Alabama. Day Care Services operates a system of day care centers and has a number of positions which would not be found in a smaller organization. A single center day care organization could adopt these materials through combining certain job duties.

Job Title: Executive Director

Responsible to: Day Care Services Board through the Executive Committee

General Duties: Responsible for the entire function of the organization.

I. Daily Duties:
  1. Receive correspondence
  2. Answer correspondence
  3. Deal with the day-to-day problems of the organization
  4. Be available to staff for consultation and advice
  5. Be available to Board
  6. Be available to local, state, federal and private agencies as pertaining to the operation of the agency
  7. Organize and direct daily operational activities
  8. Keep informed of available local, state and federal funding
II. Periodic Duties:
  1. Attendance of Executive Committee meetings
  2. Attendance of Board meetings
  3. Regular reports to Executive Committee and Board
  4. Staff meetings
  5. Submittal of reports to various state agencies

III. Occasional Duties:
  1. Attendance of conferences
  2. Attendance of meetings pertinent to the agency's role in the community
  3. Act as resource to the greater community
IV. Other Duties as Assigned

Relationships:
  1. All staff
  2. Boards
  3. Local, state and federal government agencies
  4. The greater community

Minimum Qualifications:
  1. Master's degree or equivalent in child development, social work, or related fields
  2. Two years of business experience either home owned or in position of responsibility
  3. Ability to write material in comprehensive form
  4. Ability to relate to different levels of the community's socioeconomic structure
  5. Ability to write and compile project applications and proposals

Job Title: Assistant Director

Responsible to: Executive Director

General Duties: Assist the executive director in all of the agency's functions. Responsible for all classroom programs including staff pre-service and in-service training.

I. Daily Duties:
  1. Coordinate efforts with other staff
  2. Receive and answer mail pertaining to education and as assigned

3. Monitor classrooms
4. Conduct in-service training programs using video tape equipment or contract for in-service sessions
5. Keep centers supplied with all necessary teaching equipment and supplies in line with budget

II. Periodic Duties:
   1. Attend and/or conduct staff meetings
   2. Submit reports
   3. Evaluate personnel
   4. Evaluate ongoing program

III. Occasional Duties:
   1. Attend parent meetings
   2. Attend conferences and meetings
   3. Preview educational materials
   4. Act as a resource person to the greater community

IV. Other Duties as Assigned

Relationships:
   1. All staff
   2. Children
   3. Parents
   4. Professionals
   5. Greater Community

Minimum Qualifications:
   1. Master's degree or equivalent in child development or related field
   2. Minimum of two years' work experience with the infant to 6-year age range
   3. Special courses or independent study in infant stimulation
   4. Able to write training materials
   5. Able to relate to children and adults
   6. Willing to increase knowledge in field of endeavor
   7. Must be agile enough to work with young children
   8. Able to relate to different socioeconomic stratas
   9. Must have car and able to drive

Job Title: Administrative Assistant

Responsible to: Executive Director

General Duties: Responsible for all general office functions.

I. Daily Duties:
   1. Answer and screen executive director's calls
   2. Receive, open, and handle all uncomplicated and/or routine mail and handle all uncomplicated and/or routine calls
   3. Receive payments by mail and follow them through to deposit
   5. Maintain an excellent filing system
   5. Handle all dictation from executive director
   6. Type reports for the supervisory teachers
   7. Supervise all clerical personnel

II. Periodic Duties:
   1. Notify Board members and staff of periodic meetings
   2. Compile reports as requested by executive director
   3. Make suggestions to executive director regarding office routines and office personnel

III. Occasional Duties:
   1. Attend meetings and record minutes
   2. Order all office supplies
   3. Contract for office machine repairs and maintenance
   4. Make appointments for interviews of prospective personnel

IV. Other Duties as Assigned

Relationships:
   1. All staff
   2. State, municipal and federal agencies
   3. Private agencies
   4. Day Care Services' Board members
   5. General public

Minimum Qualifications:
   1. Must be able to relate to adults on all levels of the socioeconomic structure of the community
   2. Must be able to type accurately at a speed of 55 words per minute
   3. Must be sound speller and have good working knowledge of English grammar
   4. Must be able to take shorthand at 80 words per minute
   5. Must be able to compose uncomplicated and/or routine correspondence
   6. High school graduate with five years' experience in general office work

Job Title: Social Worker

Responsible to: Executive Director

General Duties: It shall be the responsibility of the social worker to help initiate and coordinate a social work program for Day Care Services, Inc.

I. Daily Duties:
   1. Update case records
   2. Make necessary appointments

3. Make home visits
4. Help make available existing community services to families in need

II. Periodic Duties:
   1. Work with the center director and the parent group in the implementation of a meaningful parent program
   2. Attend staff meetings
   3. Contribute to newsletter

III. Occasional Duties:
   1. Attend workshops, conferences, etc.
   2. Conduct staff conferences

IV. Other Duties as Assigned

Relationships:
   1. Children in the Center
   2. All staff
   3. Families of enrollees
   4. Professional staff from other social agencies
   5. Greater community

Minimum Qualifications:
   1. Master's degree in Social Work
   2. Bachelor's degree in Sociology, with a minimum of one year's experience in field work
   3. Must have automobile available at all times

Job Title: Bookkeeper

Responsible to: Executive Director

General Duties: Responsible for maintaining books as necessitated by agency funding.

I. Daily Duties:
   1. Receive expense vouchers from program components
   2. Check for validity against approved budgets
   3. Present to executive director for signature
   4. Post all income and expense
   5. Receive fee income from program components
   6. Make deposit slips and deposit with Community Chest

II. Periodic Duties:
   1. Prepare monthly financial report for Day Care Services Board
   2. Prepare monthly expense accounts for pensions and security
   3. Prepare with executive director monthly estimated expenditure
   4. Prepare monthly food reimbursement report for USDA

   5. Prepare monthly breakdown on per child food cost broken down by Center
   6. Prepare monthly total per child cost broken down by the center

III. Occasional Duties:
   1. Prepare six-month financial report
   2. Prepare year-end financial report

IV. Other Duties as Assigned

Relationships:
   1. Central office staff
   2. Center directors
   3. Community Chest financial division
   4. Funding agencies

Minimum requirements:
   1. High school diploma
   2. Minimum of four years' experience
   3. Ability to set up and maintain books as necessitated by funding picture
   4. Ability to furnish pertinent financial facts upon request within a reasonable length of time
   5. Must be flexible to accommodate growing and changing organization
   6. Must retain a reasonable record of excellent health

Job Title: Teacher-Director (This position will be applicable to Centers having up to 50 children)

Responsible to: Executive Director

General Duties: Responsible for the overall efficient operation of the Center. Also, directly responsible as a teacher to one specific group of children and act as liaison between local Board and staff and Central Office and Center staff.

I. Daily Duties:
   1. Responsible for planning and executing lessons with a specific group of children
   2. Responsible for involving and training teacher aides
   3. Responsible for the supervision and functioning of all Center personnel
   4. Responsible for daily administrative needs of the Center
   5. Responsible for all programmatic phases of the Center's activities

II. Periodic Duties:
   1. Responsible for parent conferences
   2. Responsible for home visits under the direction and with the help of Day Care Services, Inc. social worker staff
   3. Responsible for attending staff meetings, initiating and holding Center staff

meetings, as well as parent meetings, and local Center Board meetings

4. Responsible for reports, maintaining accurate records on all enrollees, and maintaining accurate records on staff attendance
5. Responsible for the intake of fees, and all expenditures of the Center, and maintenance of accurate records on all fiscal items
6. Responsible for all purchases made on the Center level

III. Occasional Duties:
1. Responsible for dissemination of information to the parents
2. Responsible for arbitrating differences between Center personnel
3. Responsible for the overall planning and supervision of field trips
4. Responsible for securing transport in case of emergencies

IV. Other Duties as Assigned

Relationships:
1. All children enrolled in Center
2. Applicants and families receiving services through the Center
3. Day Care Services components
4. Boards
5. Outside agencies and Civic groups
6. Professional groups
7. General public

Minimum Qualifications:
1. Must love children and be able to relate to them
2. Must be able to relate to adults on all levels of the socioeconomic structure of the community
3. Must be in excellent health
4. Must be agile enough to perform job as a teacher of small children
5. Must be willing to continually increase knowledge in field of endeavor
6. Must be able to drive and have car available
7. a. Master's degree in child development, early childhood education or related fields
   b. Master's degree in elementary education with a minimum of one year's practical experience in an acceptable preschool situation
   c. Bachelor's degree in child development, early childhood, elementary education, or related fields, with a minimum of one year's practical ex-

perience in an acceptable preschool situation
   d. Bachelor's in elementary education with a minimum of one year's practical experience in an acceptable preschool situation
   e. Two years of college with a miminum of three years' practical experience in an acceptable preschool situation
   f. High School diploma with a minimum of five years' experience in an acceptable preschool situation

Job Title: Director (This position will be applicable to Centers with over 50 children)

Responsible to: Executive Director

General Duties: Responsible for the overall efficient operation of the Center and act as liaison between local Board and staff and Central Office and Center staff.

I. Daily Duties:
1. Responsible for the supervision and functioning of all Center personnel
2. Responsible for daily administrative needs of the Center
3. Responsible for all programmatic phases of the Center's activities

II. Periodic Duties:
1. Responsible for parent conferences
2. Responsible for home visits under the direction and with the help of Day Care Services, Inc. social worker staff
3. Responsible for attending staff meetings, initiating and holding Center staff meetings, as well as parent meetings, and local Center Board meetings
4. Responsible for reports, maintaining accurate records on all enrollees, and maintaining accurate records on staff attendance
5. Responsible for the intake of fees, all expenditures of the Center, and maintenance of accurate fiscal records
6. Responsible for all purchases made on the Center level

III. Occasional Duties:
1. Responsible for dissemination of information to the parents
2. Responsible for arbitrating differences between Center personnel
3. Responsible for the overall planning and supervision of field trips
4. Responsible for securing transport in case of emergencies

5. Responsible for trouble-shooting in any position in the Center in case of need.

IV. Other Duties as Assigned

Relationships
1. All children enrolled in Center
2. Applicants and families receiving services through the Center
3. Day Care Services components
4. Boards
5. Outside agencies and Civic groups
6. Professional groups
7. General public

Minimum Qualifications:
1. Must love children and be able to relate to them
2. Must be able to relate to adults on levels of the socioeconomic structure of the community
3. Must be in excellent health
4. Must be agile enough to perform job as teacher of small children
5. Must be willing to continually increase knowledge in field of endeavor
6. Must be able to drive and have car available
7. a. Master's degree in child development, early childhood education, or social work, or related fields
   .b. Master's degree in Elementary Education with a minimum of one year's practical experience in an acceptable preschool situation
   c. Bachelor's degree in Early Education, child development, early childhood, or social work, or related fields, with a minimum of one year's practical experience in an acceptable preschool situation
   d. Bachelor's degree in Elementary Education with a minimum of one year's experience in an acceptable preschool situation
   e. Two years of college with a minimum of three year's practical experience in an acceptable preschool situation
   f. High School diploma with a minimum of five years' experience in an acceptable preschool situation

Job Title: Head Teacher

Responsible to: Center Director

General Duties: Responsibility is to plan and execute an educational program in line with Day Care Services, Inc.'s educational goals and beliefs. Shall assume the director's responsibilities during the director's absence.

I. Daily Duties:
1. Responsible to greet each child in assigned group
2. Responsible for the daily planning and execution of all classroom and outdoor activities for group
3. Responsible for the welfare, health and safety of the children in group
4. Responsible for the supervision of group in the bathroom
5. Responsible for all mealtime activities of group, will eat with the children
6. Responsible for daily attendance reports of group
7. Responsible for training and constructive utilization of teacher aides

II. Periodic Duties:
1. Responsible for attending staff meetings
2. Responsible for all required reports pertaining to group
3. Responsible for holding parent conferences

III. Occasional Duties:
1. Responsible for attending workshops, conferences, all in-service training
2. Responsible for assisting other staff in cleaning Center thoroughly
3. Responsible for all Center functions in the absence of the Center director

IV. Other Duties as Assigned

Relationships:
1. Children of the Center
2. Families of enrollees
3. All Center staff
4. All Day Care Services, Inc. staff
5. Professional staff from other agencies, Institutes of Higher Learning, etc.
6. Greater community

Minimum Qualifications:
1. Must love children and be able to relate to them
2. Must be able to relate to adults on all levels of the socioeconomic structure of the community
3. Must be in excellent health
4. Must be agile enough to perform job as a teacher of small children
5. Must be willing to continually increase knowledge in field of endeavor
6. a. Bachelor's degree in child development or early childhood education, or related fields

b. Bachelor's degree in elementary education, with a minimum of one year's experience in an acceptable preschool situation

c. Two years of college with a minimum of three years' experience in an acceptable preschool situation

d. High school graduate with a minimum of five years' experience in an acceptable preschool situation

Job Title: Supervisory Teacher

Responsible to: Executive Director

General Duties: In conjunction with the assistant director the supervisory teacher will conduct an ongoing in-service program as well as a pre-service program for classroom personnel.

I. Daily Duties:
1. Coordinate efforts with other staff
2. Monitor classrooms
3. Conduct in-service training utilizing available equipment and materials
4. Assist in keeping the centers supplied with all necessary teaching equipment and supplies in line with existing budget
5. Submit written reports on monitoring visits and/or training

II. Periodic Duties:
1. Attend staff meetings
2. Submit reports
3. Assist in evaluating classroom personnel
4. Assist in evaluating the ongoing classroom program

III. Occasional Duties:
1. Attend Center Board meetings
2. Give reports to Day Care Services' Board
3. Assist in previewing educational materials
4. Act as resource person to greater community
5. Plan and execute training sessions

IV. Other Duties as Assigned

Relationships:
1. All staff
2. Children
3. Parents
4. Professional
5. Greater Community

Minimum Qualifications:
1. Master's degree or equivalent in child development or related field
2. Minimum of one year's work experience with infants to 6-year age range

3. Special courses or independent study in infant stimulation
4. Able to write training materials
5. Able to relate to children and adults
6. Willing to increase knowledge in field of endeavor
7. Must be agile enough to work with young children
8. Able to relate to different socioeconomic strata
9. Must have car and be able to drive

Job Title: Teacher

Responsible to: Center Director

General Duties: Responsible for planning and executing an educational program in line with Day Care Services, Inc.'s educational goals and beliefs.

I. Daily Duties:
1. Responsible for greeting each child in assigned group
2. Responsible for the daily planning and execution of all classroom and outdoor activities
3. Responsible for the welfare, health and safety of the children in group
4. Responsible for the supervision of group in the bathroom
5. Responsible for all mealtime activities of group, will eat with the children
6. Responsible for daily attendance reports
7. Responsible for training and constructive utilization of teacher aide

II. Periodic Duties:
1. Responsible for attending staff meetings
2. Responsible for all required reports pertaining to group
3. Responsible for holding parent conferences

III. Occasional Duties:
1. Responsible for attending workshops, conferences, all in-service training
2. Responsible for assisting other staff in cleaning Center thoroughly
3. Responsible for making home visits

IV. Other Duties as Assigned

Relationships:
1. Children in the Center
2. Families of enrollees
3. All Center staff
4. All Day Care Services, Inc. staff
5. Professional staff from other agencies, Institutes of Higher Learning, etc.
6. Greater community

Job Title: Teacher Aide

Responsible to: Teacher

General Duties: Responsible for assisting the teacher in planning and executing an educational program in line with Day Care Services' educational goals and beliefs.

I. Daily Duties:
1. Responsible for assisting in greeting each child of assigned group
2. Responsible for assisting in the daily planning and execution of all classroom and outdoor activities
3. Responsible for assisting in welfare, health, and safety of the children in group
4. Responsible for assisting in bathroom supervision
5. Responsible for assisting in all mealtime activities, will eat with the children

II. Periodic Duties:
1. Responsible for assisting in holding parent conferences
2. Responsible for attending staff meetings

III. Occasional Duties:
1. Responsible for attending workshops, conferences, all in-service training
2. Responsible for assisting other staff in cleaning Center thoroughly

IV. Other Duties as Assigned

Relationships:
1. Children of the Center
2. Families of enrollees
3. All Center staff
4. All Day Care Services, Inc. staff
5. Professional staff from other agencies, Institutes of Higher Learning, etc.
6. Greater community

Minimum Qualifications:
1. Must love children and be able to relate to them
2. Must be able to relate to adults on all levels of the socioeconomic structure of the community
3. Must be in excellent health
4. Must be agile enough to perform job as a teacher of small children
5. Must be willing to continually increase knowledge in field of endeavor
6. Must be a high school graduate

Job Title: Cook

Responsible to: Center Director

General Duties: Responsible for the preparation of foods and the cleanliness of kitchen and food storage areas.

I. Daily Duties:
1. Responsible for the preparation of lunch
2. Responsible for the preparation of snacks, though need not necessarily be present at snack time
3. Responsible for washing dishes and all utensils used in the preparation of foods
4. Responsible for the daily cleaning of counter tops and stove and daily spot cleaning of all kitchen surfaces
5. Responsible for daily mopping of kitchen floor
6. Responsible, if applicable, for the supervision and training of assistant cook

II. Periodic Duties:
1. Responsible for cleaning of refrigerator, freezer, cabinets, stove, and sterilizer
2. Responsible for kitchen equipment and food inventories
3. Responsible with the Director for adjustments of menus
4. Responsible for making shopping lists
5. Responsible to attend Center staff meeting

III. Occasional Duties:
1. Responsible for setting up tables at picnic
2. Responsible for the purchase of groceries
3. Responsible for attendance of agency staff meeting
4. Responsible for working with parents individually or in small groups on "good" nutrition
5. Responsible to attend workshops and in-service training sessions

IV. Other Duties as Assigned

Relationships:
1. Children of the Center
2. Other Center staff
3. Families of enrollees
4. State and municipal agencies
5. Other Day Care Services staff
6. Repairmen

Minimum Qualifications:
1. Must like children and be able to relate to them
2. Must be able to relate to adults
3. Must be in excellent health
4. Must be clean and neat
5. Must be willing to learn and follow instructions
6. Must be functionally literate and able to do simple arithmetic
7. Must have basic knowledge of food preparation and nutrition
8. High school education or equivalent

Job Title: Assistant Cook

Responsible to: Cook

General Duties: Responsible in assisting the cook.

I. Daily Duties:
1. Responsible for assisting in preparation of lunch
2. Responsible for assisting in preparation of snacks, though need not necessarily be present at snack time
3. Responsible for assisting in washing dishes and all utensils used in the preparation of foods
4. Responsible for assisting in the daily cleaning of counter tops, and stove, and daily spot cleaning of all kitchen surfaces
5. Responsible for assisting in daily mopping of kitchen floor

II. Periodic Duties:
1. Responsible for assisting in the cleaning of refrigerator, freezer, cabinets, stove and sterilizer
2. Responsible for assisting in the responsibility for kitchen equipment and food inventories
3. Responsible for assisting with the Director adjustment of menus
4. Responsible for assisting in the making of shopping lists
5. Responsible for attending Center staff meeting

III. Occasional Duties:
1. Responsible for assisting in the setting up of tables at picnics
2. Responsible for assisting in purchasing of groceries
3. Responsible for attendance of agency staff meeting
4. Responsible for attending workshops and all in-service training sessions
5. Responsible for assisting cook in working with parents individually or in small groups on "good" nutrition

IV Other Duties as Assigned

Relationships:
1. Children of the Center
2. Other Center staff
3. Families of enrollees
4. State and Municipal agencies
5. Other Day Care Services employees
6. Repairmen

Minimum Qualifications:
1. Must like children and be able to relate to them

2. Must be able to relate to adults
3. Must be in excellent health
4. Must be clean and neat
5. Must be willing to learn and follow instructions
6. Must be functionally literate and able to do simple arithmetic
7. Must have basic knowledge of food preparation and nutrition
8. Must have high school education or equivalent

Job Title: Housekeeper

Responsible to: Center Director

General Duties: Responsible for the cleaning of the Center facility.

I. Daily Duties:
1. Responsible for cleaning floors, before arrival of children
2. Responsible for cleaning bathroom
3. Responsible for cleaning floors and table after meals
4. Responsible for assisting in setting up of cots
5. Responsible for keeping children's washcloths, sheets, blankets, etc.
6. Responsible for spot cleaning of finger prints on woodwork and windows and walls
7. Responsible for setting tables or carrying dishes, etc. to the classroom for family style meals
8. Responsible for dusting

II. Periodic Duties:
1. Responsible for mopping and waxing floors
2. Responsible for washing furniture
3. Responsible for cleaning venetian blinds
4. Responsible for attending staff meetings

III. Occasional Duties:
1. Responsible for helping other staff supervise children on field trips
2. Responsible for assisting with parties
3. Responsible for attending workshops and in-service training

IV. Other Duties as Assigned

Relationships:
1. Children of the Center
2. Other Center staff
3. Other staff of Day Care Services, Inc.
4. Families of center enrollees
5. Merchants
6. City and state employees, e.g., fire inspector

Minimum Qualifications:
1. Must love children and able to relate to them
2. Must be able to relate to other personnel
3. Must be in excellent health
4. Eighth grade education or equivalent
5. Must be functionally literate
6. Willing and able to follow instructions
7. Willing to learn

APPENDIX F
Sample Employee Evaluation— "Performance Review"

The materials in Appendix F are from *Child Care and Development Occupations—Competency Based Teaching Modules* by Irene Rose and Mary Elizabeth White and have been reprinted with permission.

SAMPLE

PERFORMANCE REVIEW

Name_____ Position_____

	Poor	Fair	Good	Excell.	Comments
1. Attitude Toward:					
Children	___	___	___	___	_____
Parents	___	___	___	___	_____
Other staff	___	___	___	___	_____
Interns	___	___	___	___	_____
Volunteers	___	___	___	___	_____
Program	___	___	___	___	_____
2. Ability to work with others	___	___	___	___	_____
3. Responsibility when not supervised:	___	___	___	___	_____
Initiative, taking responsibility	___	___	___	___	_____
4. Adaptability:					
Changing hours	___	___	___	___	_____
Working extra hours	___	___	___	___	_____
Helping with other groups	___	___	___	___	_____
Profiting from constructive criticism	___	___	___	___	_____

	Poor	Fair	Good	Excell.	Comments
5. Performance:					
Work habits	___	___	___	___	_____
Program planning and follow-up	___	___	___	___	_____
Handling of behavior problems	___	___	___	___	_____
Playground supervision	___	___	___	___	_____
Eating supervision	___	___	___	___	_____
Toileting supervision	___	___	___	___	_____
Resting supervision	___	___	___	___	_____
Conforming to policies	___	___	___	___	_____
6. Self-development:					
Willingness to attend conferences and courses	___	___	___	___	_____
Reading and studying	___	___	___	___	_____
Ability to accept and use training	___	___	___	___	_____
Willingness to change	___	___	___	___	_____
Comprehension of day care	___	___	___	___	_____
Understanding of age levels	___	___	___	___	_____
7. Attendance	___	___	___	___	_____
8. Punctuality	___	___	___	___	_____
9. Appearance:					
Good grooming	___	___	___	___	_____
Cleanliness	___	___	___	___	_____
Voice and speech	___	___	___	___	_____

Special Improvement Needed: _____

_____

_____

Supervisor _____ Date _____

Employee's Signature _____ Date _____

Sample Employee Evaluation—

"Region III Interagency Child Development Services"

805 HAL GREER BOULEVARD
HUNTINGTON, WEST VIRGINIA 25703

STAFF EVALUATION DIRECTIONS

1. The evaluation will be completed every three months for the first year of employment and twice yearly thereafter. However, evaluations may be completed more often if a need arises.

2. Each staff member completes a self-evaluation, while the coordinator also completes one on each staff member. (In the case of aide evaluation, the coordinator works with the teacher in completing one form.) After the coordinator and the staff members have completed their forms, a conference is held to discuss and compare the results. From this discussion, goals are projected for future improvement.

3. The director and coordinator discuss staff evaluations. Completed evaluation forms are then shared with the Region III Interagency Child Development Board of Directors.

   Permission for other organizations to use evaluation forms developed for Region III ICCDS may be requested by contacting Region III office at the address shown above.

AIDE EVALUATION

NAME_____ CENTER_____ COMPLETED BY_____

RATINGS: 6. Outstanding
5. Above Average
4. Average

3. Evidence of Development
2. Needs Improvement
1. Evidence not observed or not applicable

COMPETENCY	EVIDENCE	6	5	4	3	2	1
I. Assists teacher in providing experiences which promote development for each individual	A. Makes equipment available for gross motor activities outside						
	B. Makes equipment available for gross motor activities inside						

73

COMPETENCY	EVIDENCE	6	5	4	3	2	1
	C. Encourages and assists children who need special help						
	D. Participates actively with the children						
	E. Helps to provide manipulative materials, such as puzzles, lacing boots, art materials, etc.						
II. Assists teacher in providing experiences which promote social-emotional development of each child	A. Accepts, respects, and utilizes the child's ideas						
	B. Keeps promises to child						
	C. Listens attentively without interrupting						
	D. Respects and handles children's work with care						
	E. Offers reassurance and/or empathy, when needed						
	F. Engages in meaningful verbal interaction with child frequently						
	G. Is alert to non-verbal clues						
	H. Provides a variety of opportunities to help child develop and understand appropriate relationships with others						
	I. Fosters group awareness and a feeling of belonging						
	J. Provides opportunities for child to experience activities in self-management centered around meal time						
	K. Encourages independent care of self in dressing, toileting, etc.						
	L. Fosters independence in care and use of materials and equipment						

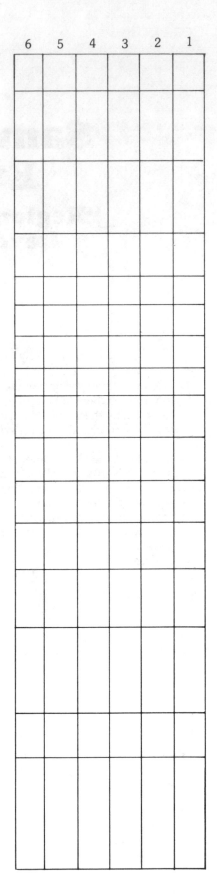

COMPETENCY	EVIDENCE	6	5	4	3	2	1
III. Assists teacher in providing experiences which promote intellectual growth and are appropriate to the stage of development of the individual child	A. Helps to provide a variety of cognitive materials which enable each child to make choices						
	B. Provides experiences which promote individual self-expression in conversation, imaginative play, and creativity						
	C. Selects appropriate books and stories						
	D. Encourages an interest in, and an enjoyment of children's literature						
	E. Assists in providing a variety of language stimulation activities, such as flannel board, puppets, finger plays, song and story records, etc.						
	F. Helps to provide and encourage experience involving thinking skills, such as generalizing, classifying, problem solving, etc.						
	H. Assists teacher in promoting conceptual development in: 1. art 2. math 3. science 4. music 5. social science						
IV. Assists teacher in providing a safe and healthy learning environment for the child	A. Is aware of, and appropriately responsive to, the health needs of the child						
	B. Recognizes and acts against hazards to safety						
V. Helps to provide a skillfully managed, child-centered environment	A. Assists teacher in implementing the routine of daily activities: 1. Anticipates the need and provides assistance in teacher-directed activities						

COMPETENCY   EVIDENCE

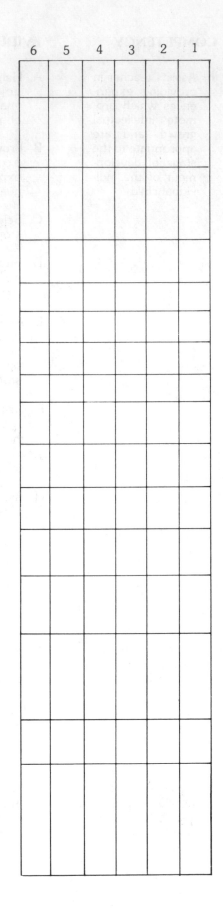

	6	5	4	3	2	1

2. Accepts responsibility in implementing small group activities, under teacher guidance

3. Accepts responsibility in skillfully managing the classroom when the teacher is absent from room

4. Takes advantage of the "teachable moment"

5. Helps effect a smooth transition from one activity to another

6. Helps supervise toileting, tooth brushing, and hand washing

7. Helps child change clothes, in case of a toileting accident

8. Helps child relax at nap time

B. Is able to plan and work cooperatively with other adults in the center

C. Provides positive guidance techniques which foster the child's ability to be self-disciplined:
   1. Guides the child in understanding and following clearly defined limits

   2. Treats behavior problems individually and privately

   3. Reinforces positive behavior and deals appropriately with negative behavior

   4. Is kind and understanding while being firm and consistent

COMPETENCY	EVIDENCE	6	5	4	3	2	1
	D. Assists in maintaining a neat, attractive room						
	E. Helps achieve a pleasant, inviting atmosphere in which the child feels comfortable and secure						
VI. Exhibits acceptable personal qualities and professional attitudes	A. Possesses the following personal attributes:						
	1. Positive self-concept						
	2. Positive in relationships with others						
	3. Reliable						
	4. Self-controlled						
	5. Sense of humor						
	6. Enthusiastic						
	7. Appropriately dressed and well-groomed						
	8. Clear, well-modulated voice						
	9. Carries out expected duties						
	10. Maintains professional behavior						
	11. Discusses concerns directly and openly with appropriate staff person						
	B. Exhibits the following professional attitudes: 1. Recognizes own strengths and weaknesses						
	2. Profits by constructive criticism						
	3. Assumes supportive functions such as: a. Strives to understand child and family						

COMPETENCY	EVIDENCE	6	5	4	3	2	1
	b. Keeps all information on children and family confidential						
	c. Participates actively in in-service training						
	d. Contributes to discussion in staff meetings						
	e. Gives assistance to teacher in maintaining current and accurate records						
	f. Realizes importance of role in classroom						
	g. Contributes to positive community-center relations						
	h. Maintains a friendly and helpful attitude toward visitors, while continuing his/her role as aide						
VII. Respects authority of teacher as supervisor of center activities	A. Sees teacher as model and follows example						
	B. Willingly accepts teacher's guidance						
	C. Follows policies set forth in staff manual						

APPENDIX H
Sample Employee Evaluation—
"California Area Family Development Center— Louisville, Kentucky"

The following is an example of an employee evaluation process based on the specific expectations written in the employee's job description. It was developed by the Community Coordinated Child Care of Louisville and Jefferson County, Louisville, Kentucky for a day care center which is a part of its system (the California Area Family Development Center, Louisville, Kentucky). For more information on this approach, contact Mrs. Patricia Murrell, Executive Director, 1355 South Third Street, Louisville, Kentucky 40208.

The documents include a general description of education and training requirements for each teaching job, a sample job description for the teacher position, a sample employee evaluation form for teacher position, and a summary form to be completed at the end of each employee evaluation.

California Area Family Development Center, Inc.

Requirements for Teachers and Assistants
1. A high school degree or the equivalent
2. Formal training in child care, such as WIN, high school training, or CDA
3. Experience in an early childhood program

Assistant Teacher
An assistant teacher will have the same general responsibilities of a teacher. In the following areas, an assistant teacher will act as a co-worker but will not have final, overall responsibility:
1. Program planning
2. Evaluation of children
3. Parent-Teacher conferences

Kindergarten Teacher
The kindergarten teacher will have the same general responsibilities of a teacher. In addition, the kindergarten teacher is responsible for planning a curriculum to meet the needs of five-year-old children.

Requirements:
1. A college degree in early childhood education or child development
2. Practicum with children
3. Preferably state certification in kindergarten

CALIFORNIA AREA FAMILY DEVELOPMENT CENTER, INC.

JOB DESCRIPTION—Teacher
A teacher has primary responsibility for planning, organizing and carrying out a developmental program for her (his) group of children.

A teacher should strive to continually develop in the following areas of responsibility:

A Teacher is Responsible for the Following Attitudes and Personal Qualities:
1. Friendliness, warmth toward people
2. A sense of humor
3. Dependability
4. Self-confidence
5. Enthusiasm about teaching
6. A desire to grow and learn
7. An ability to evaluate self
8. A clear and well-modulated voice
9. Appearance and dress that are neat and suitable for working with young children

A Teacher is Responsible for the Following Aspects of Program Development:

1. Independence in assuming responsibility
2. Efficient and satisfactory arrangement of interest areas, rooms, storage and outdoor area
3. Adjustment of temperature, light, and ventilation
4. Planning program to enrich the lives of children according to their group and individual levels of development
5. Flexibility in planning program
6. Overall planning for program on a weekly and annual basis (copy submitted to director)
7. Daily preparation of program materials; requisition of supplies as needed
8. Making teaching materials to fit program needs
9. Recording of each child's individual progress
10. Evaluation of children semi-annually
11. Conferences with parents after evaluations
12. Accurate recording of attendance
13. Carrying out procedures for emergencies and fire drills
14. Carrying out all personnel policies
15. Carrying out all policies of the parent handbook
16. Carrying out housekeeping standards
17. Carrying out procedures for outdoor play
18. Working with the parent coordinator when children have special needs
19. Working with the on-going program of parent involvement
20. Planning specific programs and projects to be completed by parent or community volunteers.
21. Active participation in staff meetings
22. Submitting articles to the newsletter
23. Discussing pertinent problems with the director
24. Professional development through reading, projects, and workshops

A Teacher is Responsible for the Following Skills in Work with Children:

1. Creating a warm and accepting environment
2. Accepting each child as he or she is
3. Recognizing that each child is a sensitive, thinking individual and treating him or her accordingly
4. Understanding the process of child development and relating that understanding to teaching
5. Showing awareness of progress or lack of it in a child's behavior
6. Dealing with children impartially
7. Being aware of the differing moods of children, adjusting standards for them at times when they are fatigued, irritated, over-stimulated
8. Using different, though consistent, methods in dealing with different children
9. Using imagination and creativity
10. Being resourceful, having common sense
11. Using a positive approach
12. Helping children accept limitations
13. Making suggestions without antagonizing
14. Not overstimulating or causing tension in children
15. Removing distracting influences
16. Being alert to the total group, even when dealing with a part of it
17. Remaining controlled in startling or difficult situations
18. Encouraging and guiding the expression of feelings, being a good listener
19. Assisting children in gaining confidence
20. Treating the child's possessions and projects with care
21. Giving children opportunity for manipulating various kinds of creative materials
22. Explaining relations between a child's individual rights and group rights
23. Guiding children in group relations
24. Guiding of activities according to group needs and interests
25. Guiding of children in developing motor coordination
26. Guiding in music experiences
27. Guiding in the development of health and safety habits
28. Guiding in language experiences
29. Guiding in math, science and problem-solving experiences
30. Guiding in use of creative materials
31. Guiding in naptime routine
32. Guiding in nutritional experiences, including family-style eating and cooking

A Teacher is Responsible for the Following Attitudes and Skills in Working with Adults:

1. Being interested in people, thinking in terms of helping them rather than criticizing
2. Cooperating
3. Being able to profit by constructive criticism and being able to give constructive criticism
4. Being a good listener
5. Being considerate of the activities of others; displays tact and courtesy
6. Accepting the overall goals shared by all for the sake of the children
7. Welcoming new ideas, flexible as shown by willingness to consider new ideas
8. Maintaining high standards of professional ethics in regard to children, parents, and staff

9. Realizing that situations cannot always be handled in the home as they are at school
10. Striving to involve parents in as many ways possible in the Center's program

CALIFORNIA AREA FAMILY DEVELOPMENT CENTER, INC.

EVALUATION OF TEACHER

Indicate evaluation by using numbers 1 through 5; 5 meaning high, appropriate, or very good; 3 average; and 1 low, inappropriate, or poor in that particular characteristic.

A teacher is responsible for the following *attitudes and personal qualities:*
____ 1. Friendliness, warmth toward people
____ 2. A sense of humor
____ 3. Dependability
____ 4. Self-confidence
____ 5. Enthusiasm about teaching
____ 6. A desire to grow and learn
____ 7. An ability to evaluate self
____ 8. A clear and well-modulated voice
____ 9. Appearance and dress that are neat and suitable for working with young children

A teacher is responsible for the following aspects of *program development:*
____ 1. Independence in assuming responsibility
____ 2. Efficient and satisfactory arrangement of interest areas, rooms, storage and outdoor area
____ 3. Adjustment of temperature, light, and ventilation
____ 4. Planning program to enrich the lives of children according to their group and individual levels of development
____ 5. Flexibility in planning program
____ 6. Overall planning for program on a weekly and annual basis (copy submitted to director)
____ 7. Daily preparation of program materials; requisition of supplies as needed
____ 8. Making teaching materials to fit program needs
____ 9. Recording of each child's individual progress
____ 10. Evaluation of children semi-annually
____ 11. Conferences with parents after evaluations
____ 12. Accurate recording of attendance
____ 13. Carrying out procedures for emergencies and fire drills
____ 14. Carrying out all personnel policies

____ 15. Carrying out all policies of the parent handbook
____ 16. Carrying out housekeeping standards
____ 17. Carrying out procedures for outdoor play
____ 18. Working with the parent coordinator when children have special needs
____ 19. Working with the ongoing program of parent involvement
____ 20. Planning specific programs and projects to be completed by parent or community volunteers
____ 21. Active participation in staff meetings
____ 22. Submitting articles to the newsletter
____ 23. Discussing pertinent problems with the director
____ 24. Professional development through reading, projects and workshops

A teacher is responsible for the following *skills in work with children:*
____ 1. Creating a warm and accepting environment
____ 2. Accepting each child as he or she is
____ 3. Recognizing that each child is a sensitive, thinking individual and treating him or her accordingly
____ 4. Understanding the process of child development and relating that understanding to teaching
____ 5. Showing awareness of progress or lack of it in a child's behavior
____ 6. Dealing with children impartially
____ 7. Being aware of the differing moods of children, adjusting standards for them at times when they are fatigued, irritated, overstimulated
____ 8. Using different, though consistent, methods in dealing with different children
____ 9. Using imagination and creativity
____ 10. Being resourceful, having common sense
____ 11. Using a positive approach
____ 12. Helping children accept limitations
____ 13. Making suggestions without antagonizing
____ 14. Not overstimulating or causing tension in children
____ 15. Removing distracting influences
____ 16. Being alert to the total group, even when dealing with a part of it
____ 17. Remaining controlled in startling or difficult situations
____ 18. Encouraging and guiding the expression of feelings; being a good listener
____ 19. Assisting children in gaining confidence
____ 20. Treating the child's possessions and projects with care
____ 21. Giving children opportunity for manipulating various kinds of creative materials

___ 22. Explaining relations between a child's individual rights and group rights
___ 23. Guiding children in group relations
___ 24. Guiding of activities according to group needs and interests
___ 25. Guiding of children in developing motor coordination
___ 26. Guiding in music experiences
___ 27. Guiding in the development of health and safety habits
___ 28. Guiding in language experiences
___ 29. Guiding in math, science and problem-solving experiences
___ 30. Guiding in use of creative materials
___ 31. Guiding in naptime routine
___ 32. Guiding in nutritional experiences, including family-style eating and cooking

A teacher is responsible for the following *skills in working with adults:*
___ 1. Being interested in people, thinking in terms of helping them rather than criticizing
___ 2. Cooperating
___ 3. Being able to profit by constructive criticism and being able to give constructive criticism
___ 4. Being a good listener
___ 5. Being considerate of the activities of others; displays tact and courtesy
___ 6. Accepting the overall goals shared by all for the sake of the children
___ 7. Welcoming new ideas, flexible as shown by willingness to consider new ideas
___ 8. Maintaining high standards of professional ethics in regard to children, parents, and staff
___ 9. Realizing that situations cannot always be handled in the home as they are at school
___ 10. Striving to involve parents in as many ways possible in the Center's program

CALIFORNIA AREA FAMILY DEVELOPMENT CENTER, INC.

Professional Development completed since the last evaluation.

Specific strengths of staff person:

Specific limitations of staff person:

Goals, recommendations for future:

Response by staff person:

I have read and understand all of the above.

Signed _____